THE OUTLINE BAR

| ← | → | ↑ | ↓ | →‖ | | + | − | Show: | 1 | 2 | 3 | 4 | 5 | 6 | 7 | 8 | 9 | All |

1 2 3 4 5   6 7   —————— 8 ——————

1. Promote   5. Body Text

2. Demote   6. Expand

3. Move Up   7. Collapse

4. Move Down   8. View Heading Level

THE PRINT MERGE BAR

| Insert Merge Field... | Edit Data File | | ✓ | ⊡→▤ | ⊡→🖨 | Data File: ORDERS.DOC
Header File: |

1   2   3   4   5

1. Insert a new merge field in main document

2. Open and edit the data file

3. Check for errors in data file and main document

4. Merge to a document file

5. Merge to print

SYBEX**LEARN FAST!**BOOKS

The SYBEX *Learn Fast!* series offers busy, computer-literate people two books in one: a quick, hands-on tutorial guide to program essentials; and a comprehensive reference to commands and features.

The first half of each *Learn Fast!* book teaches the basic operations—and underlying concepts—of the topic software. These lessons feature trademark SYBEX characteristics: step-by-step procedures; thoughtful, well-chosen examples; an engaging writing style; valuable margin notes; and plenty of practical insights.

Once you've learned the basics, you're ready to start working on your own. That's where the second half of each *Learn Fast!* book comes in. This alphabetical reference offers concise instructions for using program commands, dialog boxes, and menu options. With dictionary-style organization and headings, this half of the book is designed to give you fast access to information.

SYBEX is very interested in your reactions to the *Learn Fast!* series. Your opinions and suggestions will help all of our readers, including yourself. Please send your comments to: SYBEX Editorial Department, 2021 Challenger Dr. Alameda, CA 94501.

LEARN *Word for Windows* **FAST!**

LEARN *Word for Windows*™ **FAST!**

DOUGLAS HERGERT

SYBEX®

San Francisco · Paris · Düsseldorf · Soest

Acquisitions Editor: Dianne King
Developmental Editor: Jim Compton
Editor: David Krassner
Technical Editors: Sandra Giles and Rebecca Moore Lyles
Word Processors: Ann Dunn and Susan Trybull
Book Design and Chapter Art: Claudia Smelser
Screen Graphics: Aldo Bermudez
Typesetter: Claudia Smelser
Proofreader and Production Assistant: Lisa Haden
Indexer: Nancy Guenther
Cover Designer: Ingalls + Associates
Cover Photographer: Michael Lamott
Screen reproductions produced with Collage Plus.

To my family: Elaine, Andrew, Audrey, and Boubacar

TABLE*of*CONTENTS

PART TWO REFERENCE

PREFACE

This book shows you how to use the most important features of Word for Windows and provides continuing practical support for day-to-day word-processing tasks. Part I is a tutorial in nine lessons:

- Lesson 1, *Getting Started in Word*, introduces the Word application window—including the important new Toolbar—and guides you through the steps of creating a first document.

- Lesson 2, *Revising a Document*, teaches you the basic editing skills for replacing, deleting, moving, and copying text.

- Lesson 3, *Formatting and Printing a Document*, shows you how to improve a document's appearance with fonts, point sizes, text styles, alignments, bullets, indents, margins, and tabs. You'll also learn to print both a document and an envelope.

- Lesson 4, *Proofing a Document*, gives you a first look at Word's Spelling, Grammar, and Thesaurus tools.

- Lesson 5, *Reorganizing a Document*, demonstrates the use of sections, text columns, frames, and borders to create special visual and organizational effects.

- Lesson 6, *Adding WordArt and Pictures*, presents two versatile graphics programs that come with Word: WordArt for designing special typographical displays; and Draw for adding logos, icons, or pictures to a document.

- Lesson 7, *Creating Tables and Charts*, teaches you to arrange numeric and textual information in tables and to use Microsoft Graph for creating impressive charts from tables of data.

- Lesson 8, *Using the Print Merge Feature*, shows you how to generate personalized form letters and documents with Word's flexible but simple print-merge procedures.

- Lesson 9, *Developing Shortcuts*, introduces templates, glossary entries, macros, styles, and outlining.

Part II of this book contains nearly a hundred task-oriented reference entries with succinct, accessible information about Word's major tools and procedures. In each entry you'll find step-by-step instructions, shortcuts, examples, and tips. The goal is to help you work efficiently and effectively in Word for Windows.

ACKNOWLEDGMENTS

My sincere thanks goes to the following people: Dianne King, who first suggested the book idea; James Compton, who helped develop the concept; David Krassner, who edited the manuscript and guided it through the steps of publication; Sandra Giles and Rebecca Lyles, who reviewed the technical content; and Claudette Moore, who provided ongoing encouragement and support.

PART ONE

TUTORIAL

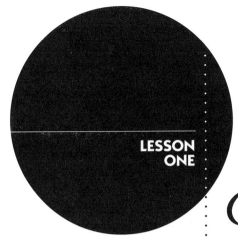

LESSON ONE

Getting Started in Word

In this first lesson you'll examine the elements of Word's *application window*. You'll start up the program and take a look at its menus, tools, and other visual elements. You'll learn how to access on-screen help for any of the features that appear in the Word window. Then you'll begin creating a sample document—a short business letter. Along the way, you'll see how to save your work regularly and how to print a copy of your document. If you have not yet installed Word for Windows on your computer, turn to the Appendix for a few simple instructions. Otherwise, the first step is to start Windows and then run Word.

STARTING WORD FOR WINDOWS

Follow these steps to get started:

1. At the DOS prompt, type **WIN** to start Windows.

2. Locate the Word program icon. If the Program Manager window is not open, double-click the Program Manager icon to open it. Then look for the Word for Windows 2.0 group. Inside the window you will find a program icon named Microsoft Word, as shown in Figure 1.1.

3. Double-click the Microsoft Word icon.

4. If Word's application window does not initially fill the screen, click the maximize button in the upper-right corner of the window.

TIP

To start both Windows and Word for Windows in a single step, simply type **WIN WINWORD** *at the DOS prompt.*

At the top of the Word application window, there is a collection of menus, buttons, and other tools, as identified in Figure 1.2. Among these lines, the *menu bar* and the *option bars* contain features you'll be using as you work on documents in Word. When you move the mouse pointer up to this area of the application window, the pointer becomes a white arrow, which you can use to select commands or tools.

A QUICK TOUR OF THE WORD APPLICATION WINDOW

When you start Word for Windows, the program opens an empty document window, where you can begin typing text. The default name for this first *active* document is simply *Document1*.

Here is a brief description of the elements in the Word window:

- The *title bar*, at the very top of the screen, contains the text *Microsoft Word-Document1*, identifying both the application and the active document.

- The *menu bar*, just beneath the title bar, contains Word's pull-down menus.

FIGURE 1.1:

The Microsoft Word program icon

◆ The *Toolbar,* beneath the menu bar, contains a unique collection of *buttons* designed to streamline operations in Word. Clicking one of these buttons is generally the same as choosing the equivalent menu command, but the Toolbar also offers a variety of important shortcuts not available elsewhere. Figure 1.3 identifies the 22 buttons in the Toolbar.

◆ The next option bar down is known as the *ribbon.* It displays options for changing the appearance of text in a document. For example, you can use the tools in this bar to select styles, fonts, point sizes, text alignments, and so on.

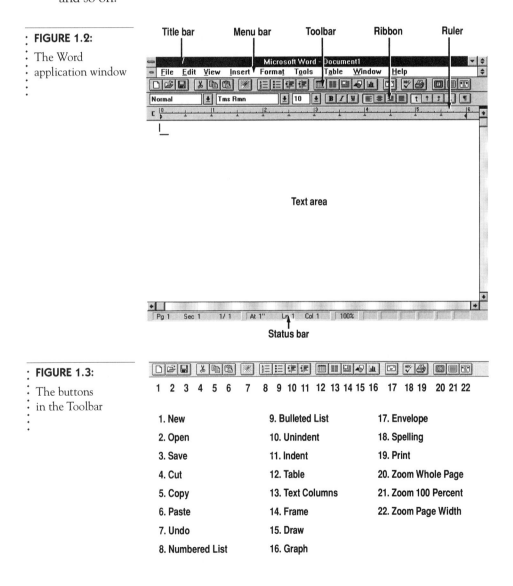

FIGURE 1.2:

The Word application window

FIGURE 1.3:

The buttons in the Toolbar

1. New	9. Bulleted List	17. Envelope
2. Open	10. Unindent	18. Spelling
3. Save	11. Indent	19. Print
4. Cut	12. Table	20. Zoom Whole Page
5. Copy	13. Text Columns	21. Zoom 100 Percent
6. Paste	14. Frame	22. Zoom Page Width
7. Undo	15. Draw	
8. Numbered List	16. Graph	

- The final option bar, just above the work area, is called the *ruler*. This bar gives you simple ways to control margins and tabs in the active document.

- The *text area* is the large empty space beneath the option bars; this is where you enter the text of your document. Initially the text area is blank except for two indicators displayed at the upper-left corner: a vertical line, called the *insertion point*; and a horizontal line, called the *end mark*. When positioned inside the text area, the mouse pointer appears as an *I-beam*, a thin vertical icon in the shape of the letter *I*. As you might expect, you can use the mouse to reposition the insertion point or to select portions of text.

- The *status bar*, at the bottom of the application window, gives you information about the active document, including the number of pages in the document, and the page you are currently working on.

*To see a quick description of any button in the Toolbar, position the mouse pointer over a button and hold down the left mouse button. The description appears in the status bar. To return to your work **without** choosing the button, move the mouse pointer back down to the text area before you release the mouse button.*

On-Line Help

Word can supply you with instant on-screen help for menu commands or other tools. Help appears in its own window, which opens whenever you request it. There are several ways to access the Word Help window. One convenient way is to use the *help pointer*. When you press Shift-F1 at the keyboard (hold down the Shift key and strike the F1 key) the mouse pointer becomes a help pointer—a white arrow alongside a bold question mark. To get help about any menu command, button, or other feature, simply click the target tool with the help pointer.

For example, suppose you want to read an explanation of the Save button, a tool you'll be using later in this lesson. Here are the steps:

1. Press Shift-F1.

2. Click the Save button, the third button from the left side of the Toolbar. The Word Help window appears on the screen, with information about saving a Word document, as shown in Figure 1.4. Click the Help window's maximize button if you want to expand the window over the entire available screen space.

3. Click the Help window's minimize button when you are finished reading the contents of the Help window.

FIGURE 1.4:

The Word
Help window

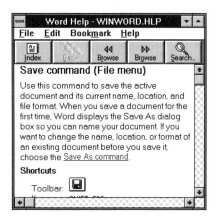

---

*Another simple way to open the Help window is to press F1 for context-sensitive help. In response, Word displays information about your current activity. For example, if you are in the middle of selecting options associated with a particular menu command, Word displays help related to that command. For more information, see the **Help** entry in **Part II**.*

MENUS AND DIALOG BOXES

As in all Windows applications, you pull down a vertical menu list by clicking its name in the menu bar. Likewise, to choose a command from the menu list, you click the command with the mouse.

In certain contexts, some menu commands are dimmed. This is Word's way of indicating that a command is not relevant to your current selection or activity, and therefore is not currently available.

Many commands are followed by ellipses (…) in their menu lists. When you choose such a command, Word displays a dialog box on the screen. As in other Windows applications, dialog boxes contain assortments of tools and controls from which you can choose options for a particular command.

To see an example of a dialog box, follow these steps:

1. Click the first name in the menu bar, File. The File menu drops down. You use commands in this menu to open a document from disk, save a document to disk, print the active document, and exit Word.

2. Click the Print command in the File menu. The Print dialog box appears
on the screen, as shown in Figure 1.5. The dialog box illustrates several different controls, all typical of dialog boxes in Windows. Here are brief
descriptions of these controls:

♦ A *drop-down list* contains options from which you can choose. To view
the list, click the down-arrow icon, found to the right of the list box.
For example, try clicking the down-arrow icon for the Print list; you'll
see a list of different parts of the active file that Word allows you to
print. (To close the list, click the down-arrow icon again.)

♦ *Option buttons* represent mutually exclusive options. For example, the
Range box in the Print dialog box contains three option buttons,
labeled All, Current Page, and Pages. To select one of these options,
you click its corresponding option button. For example, try clicking the
Current Page option. The selected option button is filled with a bold,
round bullet, and the other two options are switched off.

♦ A *check box* represents an option that you can turn on or off. A check
box containing an X is on; an empty check box is off. As you can
see, the Print dialog box contains two check boxes, called *Print to File*
and *Collate Copies*. Click either box to toggle it on or off. Unlike option
buttons, check boxes in a dialog box are controlled independently:
You can choose any combination of on and off conditions for a group
of check boxes.

♦ A *text box* is an input box where you can enter text or a numeric value.
The boxes labeled From and To are examples of text boxes in the Print
dialog box; here you can enter a range of page numbers that you wish
to print.

♦ A *command button* represents an action. You perform the action by
clicking the button. As you can see, four command buttons appear on
the right side of the Print dialog box. Almost all dialog boxes contain
OK and Cancel buttons. You click OK to confirm the current options

FIGURE 1.5:

The Print dialog box

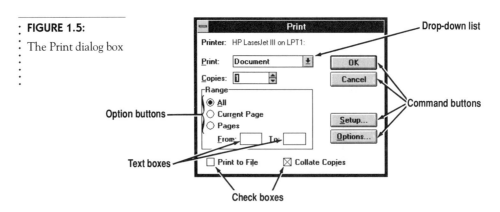

Drop-down list

Command buttons

Option buttons

Text boxes

Check boxes

and carry out the action of the command. Clicking Cancel closes the dialog box without performing any action.

3. For now, click the Cancel button to close the Print dialog box.

*If you prefer, you can use the keyboard instead of the mouse to pull down a menu list and choose a command: Press the Alt key to activate the menu bar, then press the underlined letter in a menu's name to pull down the menu. Each command in a menu list also has an underlined letter or character, which you use to choose the command. For example, with the File menu displayed, press **P** to choose the Print command. (In this book, the notation **File▶Print** means "choose the Print command from the File menu.") Within dialog boxes, you can use Alt key combinations to select options. For example, pressing Alt-E selects the Current Page option in the Print dialog box. Pressing the Enter key (represented as ⏎ in this book) is usually equivalent to clicking the OK button and pressing Esc is the same as clicking Cancel.*

With this background information, you are ready to begin typing a document.

JUST START TYPING

Figure 1.6 shows the document you'll create and work with in the remaining exercises of this lesson. It is a short letter from the owners of a bookstore to a customer who has placed a special order. As you type this letter into the Document1 text area, you'll have the opportunity to review the following special keys, which perform specific operations during text entry:

♦ You press ⏎ to complete the current paragraph and begin a new one, or to create one or more blank lines between paragraphs. Do *not* use this key to create line breaks within a paragraph. Thanks to the *word-wrap* feature, the insertion point automatically jumps down to the beginning of the next line when you reach the end of the current line in a paragraph.

♦ The Tab key moves the insertion point one tab stop forward on the current line. The default tab stops, one-half inch apart, are marked on the ruler line just above the text area.

♦ The arrow keys—represented as ↑, ↓, ←, and → in this book—move the insertion point to new positions within the text of a document. In addition, you can use Ctrl-← and Ctrl-→ to move to the previous or next word; and Ctrl-↑ and Ctrl-↓ to move the previous or next paragraph.

FIGURE 1.6:

The bookstore letter

Lantern Books
9898 Santa Barbara Avenue
San Francisco, CA 94000

2 June 1992

Ms. Jackie Alton
123 Beau Lane
Oakland, CA 94444

Dear Ms. Alton:

We are pleased to let you know that the book you ordered, Electing the American President, has finally arrived from the publisher. The price of the book is $21.95. Please stop by at your convenience and pick it up.

While you are in, you may want to browse around and see some of the other election-related titles we have recently received. Present this letter for a 10% discount on any book you decide to buy in this category. New titles include:

The 1992 Election Year
Californians and the National Election
How Women Vote

Yours sincerely,

Bill and Mary Lantern

- The Backspace key—represented as ↵ in this book—erases the character to the left of the insertion point; Ctrl-↵ erases the entire *word* to the left of the insertion point. By contrast, Del erases the character just *after* the insertion point. Ctrl-Del erases the word after the insertion point. These keys give you quick and simple ways to delete typographical errors.

- The Insert key toggles you between the *insert mode* (new text is added at the insertion point) and the *overtype* mode (new text replaces existing text at the insertion point). If you see the letters *OVR* in status bar, you are in the overtype mode; press Ins to toggle into the insert mode.

- The PgUp and PgDn keys move the insertion point one page up or down in the document. In addition, Ctrl-Home moves the insertion point back to the beginning of the document. Ctrl-End moves you to the end of the document.

Type the bookstore letter into the Document1 window, following these steps:

1. Press the Tab key five times. Then type the name of the bookstore, **Lantern Books**, and press ↵. Follow this same pattern to type the remaining two lines of the return address and the date. (Press ↵ twice after the zip code to insert a blank line before the date. After the date, press ↵ three times to insert two blank lines between the date and the customer's name.)

2. Type the three lines of text containing the customer's name and address. Press ↵ once after each of the first two lines, and twice after the third line. Type the salutation, **Dear Ms. Alton:**, and press ↵ twice.

3. Press Tab and type the first paragraph. Press ↵ twice at the end of the paragraph. Then type the remaining text of the letter: the second paragraph, the list of three additional book titles, and the closing lines. Press ↵ three times after the final title. Type five tabs before **Yours sincerely**, and press ↵ four times before typing the names of the bookstore owners.

4. Proofread your work carefully. If you find a typographical error, use the mouse or the arrow keys to move the insertion point to the position of the error, and make any necessary deletions or insertions.

When you finish, your document should look approximately like Figure 1.6. The paragraphs may be formatted somewhat differently in your copy of the letter. In the upcoming exercises you'll learn to save your work to disk and print the document.

SAVING AND PRINTING YOUR WORK

As in any other software environment, you should save your work frequently in Word to avoid major losses in the event of a power failure or other mishap. The Save button, which you examined briefly earlier in this lesson, is a convenient one-click tool for saving the active document. The first time you click this button for a new document, Word displays the Save As dialog box, shown in Figure 1.7. In this dialog box you enter a name for your new file and, optionally, specify a drive and directory location for the file (a path).

*Name your Word documents following the DOS rules for file names. The first part of the name consists of up to eight characters. By default, Word adds the extension .DOC. For example, if you enter BOOKLETR as the name of a document, the file name becomes BOOKLETR.DOC. See **Saving** in **Part II** for more information.*

Follow these steps to save the bookstore letter to disk and then to print the document:

1. Click the Save button with the mouse.

2. In the File Name text box of the Save As dialog box, enter the name **BOOKLETR**.

3. If you wish, use the Directories list box to select a directory location for the new file. Double-click the target directory's name with the mouse.

FIGURE 1.7:

The Save As
dialog box

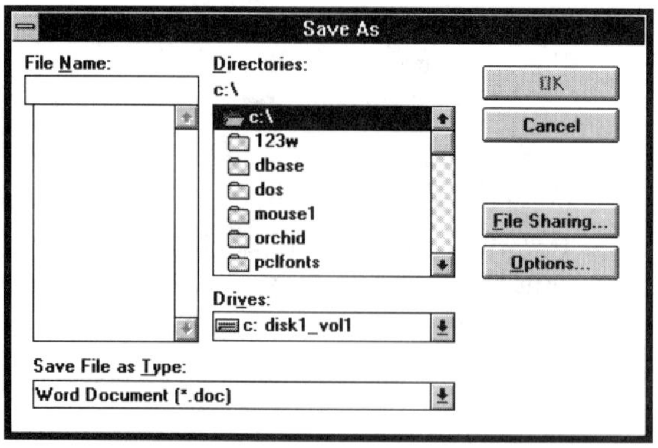

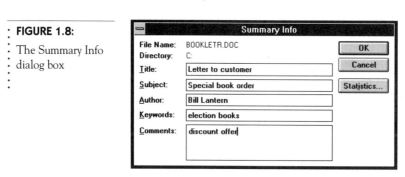

You can also select a new disk-drive destination by making a selection
from the drop-down list labeled Drives

4. Click the OK button. A new dialog box named Summary Info appears on
the screen. You use the five text boxes in this dialog box to store specific
information about your document. For this letter, enter the brief lines
of text shown in Figure 1.8. (The Author entry appears as your own
name.) As you'll learn in *Lesson 2*, this Summary Info box can help you
identify a file when you later want to reopen a document.

5. Click the OK button on the Summary Info dialog box. Now the bookstore
letter is saved on disk as BOOKLETR.DOC.

6. Make sure your printer is on and ready to operate. Click the Print button,
the fourth button from the right side of the Toolbar. (This button is a
shortcut for the File ➤ Print command; pressing the button bypasses the
File Print dialog box.)

After you have saved your document, the new name appears in the title bar of the
Word application window. Whenever you subsequently want to *update* your file—
replacing the current saved version with the latest version of your document—you
can simply click the Save button again.

FIGURE 1.8:

The Summary Info
dialog box

EXITING WORD

Now that you have completed your letter and the document is safely stored on disk, you can end this first session with Word:

1. Pull down the File menu by clicking File in the menu bar.

2. Click the Exit command. Because you have already saved the active document to disk, the current Word session ends immediately.

*If an unsaved document is open when you choose the File ➤ Exit command, Word displays a dialog box to elicit your instructions. Click Yes to save the document before exiting or No to abandon the document and exit Word. Click Cancel to return to your document in Word. See **Exiting** in **Part II** for more information.*

SUMMARY

The menu bar, Toolbar, ribbon, and ruler supply you with the tools you use to perform all variety of operations in Word. Below the option bars is the text area, where you enter and edit a document.

When you click the Save button for the first time, the Save As dialog box appears on the screen, eliciting a file name for your document. As you make subsequent changes in the document, you can update your file by clicking the Save button again. Clicking the Print button is a quick way to print a copy of the active document.

Your first step in *Lesson 2* will be to start up Word again and reopen BOOKLETR.

REFERENCE ENTRIES

To learn more, see the following entries in the reference section of this book:

- *Exiting*
- *Help*
- *Printing*
- *Ribbon*
- *Ruler*
- *Saving*
- *Toolbar*

LESSON
TWO

REVISING A DOCUMENT

Once you complete the first draft of a document, you may want to revise the text in a variety of ways, such as: Deleting unwanted text and inserting new text in its place; moving sections of text from one position to another in the document; copying text from one place to another; replacing all instances of a given character, word, or phrase with a new string of text. As you revise the bookstore letter in this lesson, you'll practice using Word's tools for these operations. For many revisions, you first need to select text—that is, to highlight a portion of text in the active document.

In Word's "select, then do" model, a selected block of text becomes the object of the next operation you perform. Word provides a variety of simple mouse and keyboard techniques for selecting different-sized portions of text—a single word, a line, a sentence, a paragraph, or the entire document.

The first step ahead of you is to reopen the BOOKLETR.DOC file. Start up Windows and Word now if you have not already done so.

FINDING AND OPENING A FILE

To open a file stored on disk, you click the Open button (the second button in the Toolbar) and then you generally select a file name from the list of DOC files displayed in the Open dialog box. Up to now you've saved only one file, but over time you'll create many Word documents and store them on your hard disk. Given a long list of file names, you may sometimes have trouble remembering what each file contains. To save you the trouble of having to open files in order to view their contents, Word has a special Find File dialog box that you can access directly from the Open dialog box. In the following steps you'll take the opportunity to examine both the Open and Find File commands as you open the BOOKLETR.DOC file:

1. Click the Open button. (Alternatively, you can choose File ➤ Open.) If necessary, use the Directories list and the Drives drop-down list to locate the BOOKLETR.DOC file. When you find the appropriate path, the File Name list appears as shown in Figure 2.1. (If you have saved the file in the WINWORD directory, there will also be some sample files, which Word places there during installation.) At this point you could open BOOK-LETR by selecting it and clicking OK; but instead, you'll take a brief detour into the Find File option.

2. Click the Find File button at the right side of the Open dialog box. In the resulting Find File dialog box, the File Name list again displays the names of documents stored in the current directory. As shown in Figure 2.2, the

FIGURE 2.1:

The Open dialog box

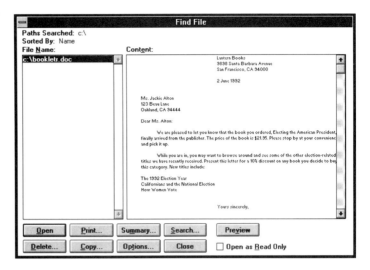

Content box displays the text of the document currently selected in the
File Name list, BOOKLETR.DOC. If there were a long list of files in the
current directory, you could view the contents of any of them simply by
selecting its name in the list.

3. Click the Summary button, near the bottom of the Find File dialog box. In
response, Word displays the Summary Info box that you prepared for this
file. (Turn back to Figure 1.8 to review this dialog box.) This is another
tool you can use to determine the context and purpose of a given file.
Click Cancel when you have finished viewing the Summary Info box.

4. Be sure BOOKLETR is highlighted and click the Open button in the Find
File dialog box. Word opens BOOKLETR, and the document appears in
the text area.

*If you want to open a file that you have worked with in a recent Word session, you
may be able to select it directly from the File menu. Pull down the File menu and look
at the bottom of the list of commands. Word displays the names of up to four files—the
documents you have most recently saved and closed. To open one of these files, simply
choose it from the list. For more information, see the entries **Saving** and **Opening a File**
in **Part II**.*

CHANGING THE
VIEW OF THE DOCUMENT

Word gives you several ways to view the current document. The default view is
called Normal. (Unless you have already changed this default, you are now looking

at the bookstore letter in Normal view.) Depending on the complexity and length of a document, some view options may be clearer or more efficient than others. These options are listed in the View menu, as you'll see in this brief exercise:

1. Pull down the View menu. The first four commands in this menu represent Word's major view options. A bullet appears next to the current view selection, Normal.

2. Choose Draft, the fourth command in the menu list. When you do so, Word changes the font of your document in the text area. The Draft option, available only in Normal view, is the most efficient way of working with complex documents.

3. Next, choose View ➤ Page Layout. This option shows you your document as it will appear on the printed page. Scroll through the document and notice that you can see the actual frame of the page. For a long and complex document this view is less efficient than Normal view. But for the one-page bookstore letter, Page Layout view is perhaps the clearest choice.

---

*Word also has the special Outline view, useful for planning long documents. For more information about views, see the entries **Normal View**, **Page Layout Mode**, and **Draft Mode** in **Part II**.*

THE SHOW/HIDE ¶ BUTTON

Your document includes certain special nonprinting characters that do not normally appear in the text area. These include tabs, paragraph marks (¶), and space marks. When you are revising text, it is sometimes useful to see these special characters so you can easily delete them or insert text between them.

To view special characters, you click the Show/Hide button, the last button at the right side of the ribbon. In the following steps you'll choose this option and then delete some of the tabs you entered in the first version of the bookstore letter:

1. Click the Show/Hide button. Word displays the special characters in your document, as shown in Figure 2.3. Tabs are represented by right-arrow symbols, and paragraph marks (¶) appear at positions where you pressed ↵ in your document. A dot represents each space character in the text.

2. Make sure the insertion point is at the very beginning of the letter. (If necessary, press Ctrl-Home to move it there.) Then press Del five times to delete the five tabs before first line of the return address. The right-arrow symbols disappear from the line, and the text *Lantern Books* moves back to the left margin.

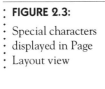

FIGURE 2.3:

Special characters
displayed in Page
Layout view

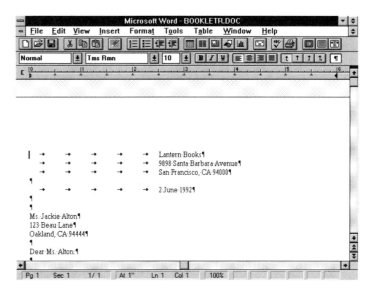

3. Delete the tabs in front of the remaining two lines of the return address and in front of the date. (You are deleting the tabs now because in *Lesson 3* you will center these lines on the page.)

4. Now click the Show/Hide button again. The special characters disappear from view.

SELECTING TEXT

For revisions such as moving, copying, deleting, or replacing text, you typically begin by selecting the words, lines, sentences, or paragraphs that you want to change. As shown in Figure 2.4, Word highlights a selection by displaying the text in white letters against a black background.

There are a variety of keyboard and mouse techniques for selecting text. Significantly, the text area of the application window contains a special column called the *selection bar*. The selection bar is an unmarked area just to the left of the text of your document. When you move the mouse pointer to the selection bar, the pointer becomes a white arrow pointing up and to the right. The selection bar is important when you want to select text with the mouse.

Some of the simplest techniques for selecting text involve the mouse, the keyboard, and the selection bar:

- ◆ To select a single word, position I-beam mouse pointer over the word and double-click the left mouse button.

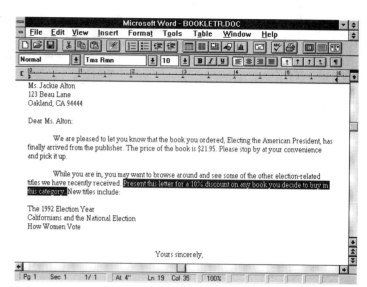

FIGURE 2.4:

A selection of text in the bookstore letter

- To select a contiguous sequence of *words*, drag the I-beam pointer over the words.

- To select an entire sentence, hold down the Ctrl key while you click the mouse anywhere in the target sentence.

- To select a single line of text, click the mouse pointer in the selection bar, just to the left of the target line.

- To select a sequence of lines, drag the mouse pointer down the selection bar in front of the lines.

- To select a paragraph, double-click the mouse pointer in the selection bar, anywhere to the left of the paragraph.

- To select all text in the active document, hold down the Ctrl key and click the mouse anywhere in the selection bar.

*To select text with the keyboard alone, you generally use the Shift key along with arrow keys or other special keys. The text you select depends upon the current position of the insertion point. For example, press Shift-↑ to select the text to the left of the insertion point on the current line and to the right of the insertion point on the line above. You can also press F8 one or more times to extend a selection: once to toggle into the extend mode; twice to select a word; three times to select a sentence; and so on. (Press Esc to toggle out of the extend mode.) For a complete list of keyboard selection techniques, choose Help ➤ Help Index, choose Keyboard and Mouse from the main index, and then choose Selecting text using keys from the subindex. Also see the entry **Selecting Text** in **Part II** of this book.*

In the following steps you'll practice some selection techniques as you make a few simple revisions to your bookstore letter:

1. Double-click over the word *pleased* in the first sentence of the first paragraph. Type the word **happy**. The new text replaces the highlighted text.

2. Double-click over the word *finally* in the same sentence. Press Del. The highlighted word is deleted from the text. Notice that Word automatically reformats the paragraph.

3. Position the mouse pointer within the final sentence of the first paragraph. Hold down the Ctrl key and click the left mouse button to select the sentence. Type this new sentence:

   Stop by to pick it up as soon as you can; we will hold it for three weeks.

   The new text replaces the old.

MOVING AND COPYING TEXT

In Version 2 of Word for Windows, moving text from one place to another in a document is easier than ever: You begin by selecting the text that you want to move, then you drag it to its new position. Alternatively, you can use the Cut and Paste buttons in the Toolbar to move text by first transferring it to the Clipboard. But for short moves within a single document, the *drag-and-drop* technique is the simplest.

DRAG-AND-DROP MOVEMENT

Follow these steps to move a sentence from the second paragraph to the end of the letter:

1. Select the second sentence in the second paragraph—the sentence that begins *Present this letter for a 10% discount.*

2. Move the mouse pointer anywhere within the highlighted sentence. The shape of the mouse pointer changes from an I-beam to a white arrow pointing up and to the left.

3. Hold down the left mouse button. The shape of the pointer changes again; behind the stem of the white arrow there is now a gray rectangle, representing the block of text you are about to drag to its new position.

4. Drag the mouse pointer down to the blank line just above the text *Yours sincerely.* As you do so, a gray insertion point moves down the document with the mouse pointer and settles at the beginning of the blank line.

5. Release the mouse button. The selected sentence moves down to its new place near the end of the letter.

6. Press the End key; this deselects the sentence and moves the insertion point to the end of the current line. Press ↵ to insert a blank line between the sentence and *Yours sincerely.*

THE CUT, COPY, AND PASTE BUTTONS

The Cut, Copy, and Paste buttons (or their equivalent commands in the Edit menu) work the same as in any other Windows application:

- The Cut button erases the selected text and transfers a copy of it to the Clipboard.

- The Copy button copies the selected text to the Clipboard, without erasing the text.

- The Paste button copies the contents of the Clipboard to the current location of the insertion point. You click the Paste button after you have already performed a Cut or Copy operation.

In the end result, a cut and paste is equivalent to a drag-and-drop. In general, you'll cut and paste when you need to move a selection of text to a distant location in the current document, or to any location in a different document. (Drag-and-drop cannot transfer text from one document to another.)

*A cut and paste procedure leaves a copy of the target text in the Clipboard. After pasting the text to one new location, you can paste a second copy to another location if you wish. By contrast, drag-and-drop does not employ the Clipboard at all. For more information, see **Moving Text** in **Part II**.*

Try the following exercise with the Cut, Copy, and Paste buttons:

1. Select the line of text that contains the book title *Californians and the National Election.* (Make sure you select the entire line by clicking in the selection bar.)

2. Click the Cut button. The title disappears from the document.

3. Move the insertion point to the beginning of the line containing the text *The 1992 Election Year*.

4. Click the Paste button. The title that was previously in the middle of the list is now at the beginning.

5. Press Ctrl-Home to move the insertion point to the beginning of the letter, and select the first line of the return address, Lantern Books.

6. Click the Copy button.

7. Press Ctrl-End to move to the end of the letter. Press ↵ to insert a new line at the end of the document. Then press Tab five times.

8. Click the Paste button. Word copies the name of the bookstore to the bottom of the document.

REPLACING TEXT

Finally, you can use Edit ➤ Replace to replace all instances of a given word or phrase with a different piece of text. Here's a brief exercise with this command:

1. Choose Edit ➤ Replace. In the resulting dialog box, enter the word **titles** in the Find What text box, and the word **books** in the Replace With text box. At this point the Replace dialog box appears as shown in Figure 2.5.

2. Click the Replace All button. Word makes the replacements and displays the message *2 changes* in the status bar. If you have started at the bottom of the document, answer Yes to the dialog box that appears.

3. Click the Close button in the Replace dialog box. The second paragraph in the letter now appears as:

   While you are in, you may want to browse around and see some of the other election-related books we have recently received. New books include:

FIGURE 2.5:

The Replace dialog box

Replace	
Fi**n**d What: `titles`	**Find Next**
	Replace
Re**p**lace With: `books`	**Replace A**ll
	Cancel
☐ Match **W**hole Word Only ☐ Match **C**ase	
— Replace with Formatting —	
Clear **Ch**aracter... **Paragraph**... **Styles**...	

*Word's Replace command is extremely versatile and powerful. For example, you can use it to replace styles as well as text. See **Replacing Text and Styles** in **Part II** for more information.*

THE UNDO BUTTON

Sometimes you may perform a revision, only to decide that you prefer the original text. Restoring the previous version of the text is easy: Just click the Undo button, the seventh button in the Toolbar. Try it now:

1. Click the Undo button.

2. Scroll down to the second paragraph of the letter, and notice that Word has undone the Replace operation you just performed.

3. Click the Save button to save the new version of the bookstore letter to disk. The current text of the letter appears in Figure 2.6.

SUMMARY

For most revisions, Word operates on a "select, then do" model: You first select the text that you want to revise, then you perform the revision. This pattern applies to

· FIGURE 2.6:

· The revised
· bookstore letter

Lantern Books
9898 Santa Barbara Avenue
San Francisco, CA 94000

2 June 1992

Ms. Jackie Alton
123 Beau Lane
Oakland, CA 94444

Dear Ms. Alton:

We are happy to let you know that the book you ordered, Electing the American President, has arrived from the publisher. The price of the book is $21.95. Stop by to pick it up as soon as you can; we will hold it for three weeks.

While you are in, you may want to browse around and see some of the other election-related titles we have recently received. New titles include:

Californians and the National Election
The 1992 Election Year
How Women Vote

Present this letter for a 10% discount on any book you decide to buy in this category.

Yours sincerely,

Bill and Mary Lantern
Lantern Books

a range of operations, such as deleting or retyping text, moving text to a new location, or copying text from one place to another.

The "select, then do" model is also important in applying formats to a document, as you'll learn in *Lesson 3*.

REFERENCE ENTRIES

For more information about the procedures covered in this lesson, see these entries in the reference section:

- *Copying Text*
- *Moving Text*
- *Opening a File*
- *Replacing Text and Styles*
- *Selecting Text*
- *Undoing an Operation*

FORMATTING AND PRINTING A DOCUMENT

Before printing the final version of the bookstore letter, you can improve its appearance and presentation in several important ways. In this lesson you'll apply *formats* and *styles* to selections of text in the document. You'll learn to do the following: Specify the *font, point size, text alignment*, and *margins* for the entire document; change *alignments* and *indentations* in selected lines and paragraphs; apply styles such as *bold* and *italics* to selected words.

Once again, you'll follow Word's "select, then do" method to make many of these changes. When all the changes are finished, you'll learn more about Word's printing features, including a special tool for printing envelopes.

Start Word now if you haven't already, and open the BOOKLETR.DOC file.

APPLYING FORMATS

The *ribbon* provides an assortment of tools designed to streamline your work with formats and styles. As you can see in Figure 3.1, the ribbon contains three boxes (actually, drop-down lists) followed by several groups of buttons. Here are brief descriptions of the options you can select from the ribbon:

- The Style box offers a list of named *styles* that you can apply to selected text in your document. A style is a group of formats identified by a name in the style list. You can create styles of your own or you can use Word's predefined styles. You'll learn to use styles in *Lesson 9*.

- The Font box contains the list of screen and printer fonts available in your installation of Windows. The selection of fonts in this list depends on both the software you have installed and the capabilities of your printer. Each font is a distinctive visual type style that you can apply to the text in a document. The default font is commonly Tms Rmn, or Times Roman, or some other *serif* font.

- The Points box lists the standard point sizes available for the selected font. You make a selection from this list when you want to increase or decrease the size of the text in your document. The default point size is 10. There are 70 points in an inch, and Word offers point sizes from 4 to 127.

- The Bold, Italics, and Underline buttons apply specific styles to a selection of text. You can apply these options individually or in combinations. Each of these buttons is a toggle: Click once to apply the style and click again to remove it.

- The alignment buttons give you a choice of four paragraph alignments on the page: left-aligned, centered, right-aligned, or justified.

FIGURE 3.1:

The ribbon

Normal	Tms Rmn	10	B I U			
1	2	3	4	5	6	7

1. Style box   5. The alignment buttons

2. Font box   6. The tab buttons

3. Points box   7. The Show/Hide button

4. The Bold, Italics, and Underline buttons

- ◆ The tab buttons allow you to set four varieties of tabs: left-aligned, centered, right-aligned, or decimal. The position of a new tab is marked on the ruler, as you'll see later in this lesson.

- ◆ Finally, the Show/Hide button displays or hides special characters, as you learned in *Lesson 2*.

In the upcoming exercises you'll use these tools to make a variety of changes in the bookstore letter.

FONTS AND POINT SIZES

One of the distinct visual characteristics of a font is the presence or lack of *serifs*, the small horizontal strokes that appear at the tops and bottoms of letters in some fonts. Times Roman contains serifs. By contrast, Helvetica is an example of a sans serif font—without serifs. Figure 3.2 shows examples of text printed in these two different fonts.

In the following exercise, you'll experiment with changes in the font and point size of the bookstore letter:

1. Select the entire text of the document by holding down the Ctrl key and clicking inside the selection bar.

2. Click the down-arrow icon to the right of the Font box in the ribbon. Scroll up and down the list to examine the selection of fonts available to you. Then choose Helvetica, or Helv, from the list. Word applies the font to the entire document.

3. Change the font back to Times Roman again, if you wish. (The letter appears in Times Roman throughout this lesson.)

FIGURE 3.2:

Examples of
Times Roman and
Helvetica fonts

Times Roman

While you are in, you may want to browse around and see some of the other election-related titles we have recently received. New titles include:

- • *Californians and the National Election*   *$7.45*
- • *The 1992 Election Year*   *$19.95*
- • *How Women Vote*   *$9.95*

Helvetica

While you are in, you may want to browse around and see some of the other election-related titles we have recently received. New titles include:

- • *Californians and the National Election*   *$7.45*
- • *The 1992 Election Year*   *$19.95*
- • *How Women Vote*   *$9.95*

4. Click the down-arrow icon to the right of the Points box. Choose 12 as the new point size.

*You can use the keyboard to make selections from the Font and Points boxes. Press Ctrl-F to activate the Font box, or Ctrl-P to activate the Points box, then press Alt-↓ to view the corresponding drop-down list. Another alternative for changing the point size of a selection is to press Ctrl-F2 for a larger size or Shift-Ctrl-F2 for a smaller size. For more information, see the **Fonts** and **Point Size** entries in **Part II**.*

BOLD, ITALICS, AND UNDERLINING

Within the context of a particular font and point size, you can apply a variety of type styles to selections of text in your document—including bold, italics, and single or double underlining. For example, try the following changes in the bookstore letter:

1. Select the first line of the document, which contains the name of the bookstore. Click the Bold button (or press Ctrl-B) and then click the Underline button (or press Ctrl-U). Activate the Points box and enter 14 as the new point size for this first line. The bookstore name now appears in bold underlined text and slightly larger than the rest of the letter.

2. Select the book title *Electing the American President*, in the first paragraph of the letter. Click the Bold and Italics buttons.

3. Select all three lines in the list of titles beneath the second paragraph. Click the Italics button.

When you want to experiment with typographical effects before applying them to your document, choose Format ➤ Character. As you can see in Figure 3.3, the

FIGURE 3.3:
The Character dialog box

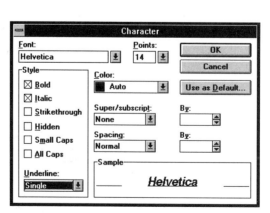

Character dialog box contains a Sample box that shows exactly what the text will look like as you make changes in the font, point size, and styles.

ALIGNMENT AND BULLETS

The text of the bookstore letter is currently aligned down the left margin of the document. Under this default alignment, lines of text break at uneven points along the right side of the document. This unjustified right margin is sometimes known as *ragged right*. In the following steps, you'll make several changes in the alignment and arrangement of the text. First you'll justify the entire document along both margins. Then you'll center the return address and date at the top of the page. Finally, you'll add *bullets* to the list of titles beneath the second paragraph:

1. Select the entire text of the document.

2. Click the Justify button (the last of the four alignment buttons) or press Ctrl-J. Word reformats the paragraphs so that lines break evenly along the right margin.

3. Select the first five lines of the document, which contain the return address, a blank line, and the date.

4. Click the Center button (the second of the four alignment buttons) or press Ctrl-E. Click elsewhere in the letter to deselect the text. Figure 3.4 shows the top half of your document at this point.

5. Move the insertion point to the position just before the word *book* in the final sentence of the letter. Insert the word **additional**. Notice that Word automatically reformats the paragraph as justified text.

FIGURE 3.4:

Centered and justified text

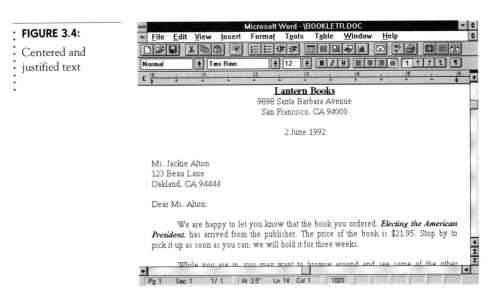

6. Select the three-line list of books beneath the second paragraph. Click the Bulleted List button, the ninth button in the Toolbar. Word inserts a bullet before each title in the list, as shown in Figure 3.5.

You can also change the spacing between lines in a document (the leading). Select the portion of the text that you want to change and press Ctrl-2 for double-spaced lines or Ctrl-5 for 1 ½-spaced lines. Press Ctrl-1 to return to single spacing. For more information, see the **Formatting Paragraphs** *entry in* **Part II***.*

SETTING INDENTS, TABS, AND MARGINS

You use the ruler to establish paragraph indents, tab stops, and margins. The ruler can display any of three different scales:

- The *paragraph scale*, shown in Figure 3.6, is the default. This scale displays paragraph indent settings and tab stops. At the left side of the paragraph scale are the left-indent markers, two small black triangles, one on top of the other. At the right side is the right-indent marker. You can reposition these indent markers along the scale when you want to display a selected paragraph within a smaller or larger horizontal width than the rest of the document.

- The *margin scale* appears when you click the *margin-scale symbol* ([ ) displayed to the left of the paragraph scale. (When you do so, the symbol is replaced by the *paragraph-scale symbol*, the two left-indent markers. Click

FIGURE 3.5:

A bulleted list

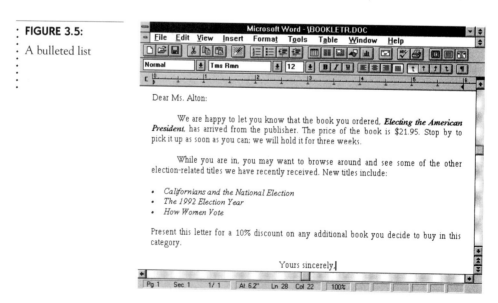

the paragraph-scale symbol to return to the paragraph scale.) As shown in Figure 3.7, the margin scale contains left- and right-margin markers that you can drag across the ruler.

- The *table scale* appears in the ruler when the insertion point is in a *table*. You'll learn about tables in *Lesson 7*.

*The ruler's paragraph and margin scales present shortcuts for three different commands in the Format menu: the Paragraph command, for creating paragraph indents; the Tabs command, for setting tabs; and the Page Setup command, for changing margins. To read more about these commands, see **Formatting Paragraphs**, **Tabs**, and **Margins** in **Part II**.*

PARAGRAPH INDENTS

You can drag both of the left-indent markers across the ruler together, or each independently, to change the left indent for the current paragraph. The position of the upper marker determines the indent of the paragraph's first line; and the position of the lower marker determines the indent of the remaining lines:

- Drag the lower marker to move both markers at once.
- Drag the upper marker to move it by itself.
- Hold down the Shift key and drag the lower marker to move it by itself.

You may have noticed that Word resets these markers automatically when you click the Bulleted List button. To see these settings, move the insertion point down to the list of titles in the bookstore letter; in the ruler, the first-line indent is at the left margin, represented as 0 in the paragraph scale. The indent for the paragraph is ¼″ from the left margin. (See *Hanging Indents* in *Part II* for more information.)

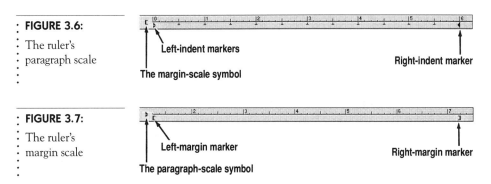

FIGURE 3.6:
The ruler's paragraph scale

Left-indent markers

Right-indent marker

The margin-scale symbol

FIGURE 3.7:
The ruler's margin scale

Left-margin marker

Right-margin marker

The paragraph-scale symbol

In the following steps you'll establish a new left indent for the bulleted list:

1. Make sure the paragraph scale is displayed on the ruler. (If the margin scale is displayed, click the paragraph-scale symbol.)

2. Select the three lines of the bulleted list.

3. In the ruler, drag the lower of the two left-indent markers to the right, stopping at the 1″ mark. Notice that the upper indent marker moves along with the lower, but the ¼″ distance between them is maintained. When you release the mouse button, the three lines of the bulleted list move over to their new left indent.

TAB STOPS

To set a new tab for a selection of lines in your document, you first click one of the four tab buttons on the ribbon and then click the position for the new tab on the ruler's paragraph scale. For example, in the following exercise you'll create a decimal tab stop in the bulleted list of books, then you'll insert the price for each book:

1. Select the three lines of the bulleted list if they are not already selected.

2. Click the Decimal-Indent Button, the second-to-last button on the ribbon.

3. Click the 4″ mark along the paragraph scale of the ruler. In response, Word clears all the default tabs to the left of this position and displays a decimal tab marker at the 4″ position.

4. Position the insertion point at the end of the first book title in the bulleted list. Press Tab and type **$7.45** as the price of the book. Word aligns the decimal point at the tab stop; the dollar digit appears to the left of the tab and the cent digits appear to the right.

5. Follow the same procedure to insert the following prices for the next two books in the list: **$19.95** and **$9.95**. The result is a column of decimal-aligned prices, displayed just to the right of the book list.

MARGINS

By default, Word sets both the left and right margins of a document at 1 ¼″. For a short document like the bookstore letter, you might want to increase the margins a little so that the text will come closer to filling the vertical length of the page. In the following steps you'll increase both margins by ¼″:

1. Click the margin scale symbol on the ruler.

2. Drag the left-margin marker ¼″ to the right, establishing the new right margin at 1 ½″.

3. Drag the right-margin marker ¼″ to the left, setting the new left margin at the 7″ mark. (Because the width of the paper is 8 ½″, this creates a left margin width of 1 ½″.)

4. Click the Save button on the Toolbar to save the latest version of this document to disk.

*These new margin settings apply to the entire text of the letter; you do not have to begin by selecting the text. However, in a document that is divided into **sections**, you can set the margins independently for each section. You'll learn about sections in **Lesson 5**.*

PREVIEWING AND PRINTING THE DOCUMENT

The File ➤ Print Preview command gives you the opportunity to see how your document will look on the printed page. In addition, you can use this command to make final adjustments to the margins before you actually print. In the following steps you'll examine the bookstore letter in the Print Preview window and you'll move the top margin to center the letter vertically on the page:

1. Choose File ➤ Print Preview. The resulting window shows a page with the text of the bookstore letter.

2. Click the Margins button at the top of the window. In response, Word draws gray lines down the length and across the width of the page to represent the current margins. As you see in Figure 3.8, each margin line has a handle, a small black square that you can drag with the mouse.

3. Position the mouse pointer over the handle for the top margin. The pointer changes to a cross hair. Drag the handle down; as you do so, the new numeric setting for the top margin appears near the top-right corner of the preview window. Drag the margin down to a setting of 2″, and then release the mouse button. Click the Margin button again; the margin lines disappear and the text moves to its new position.

FIGURE 3.8:

The Print Preview window with margin lines

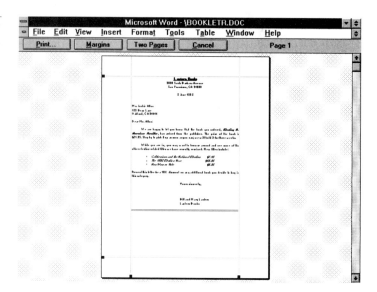

4. Click the Print button. The Print dialog box appears. If you wish to print two copies of the letter—one to send, and one to keep for your files— enter 2 into the Copies box. Click OK to print the document. The final printed copy is shown in Figure 3.9.

5. Click the Close button in the Preview window, then click the Save button in the Toolbar to save the document with its new margins.

THE ENVELOPE BUTTON

As a final exercise with this letter, you might want to try printing an envelope:

1. In the text of the letter, select the three lines containing the customer's name and address.

2. Click the Envelope button on the Toolbar. In the Create Envelope dialog box, the customer's name and address appear in the Addressed To box, as shown in Figure 3.10.

3. Feed an envelope into your printer and click the Print Envelope button. Word prints the envelope for you.

See **Printing Envelopes** in **Part II** for more information about envelopes and return addresses.

FIGURE 3.9:

The final copy of the bookstore letter

Lantern Books
9898 Santa Barbara Avenue
San Francisco, CA 94000

2 June 1992

Ms. Jackie Alton
123 Beau Lane
Oakland, CA 94444

Dear Ms. Alton:

We are happy to let you know that the book you ordered, ***Electing the American President***, has arrived from the publisher. The price of the book is $21.95. Stop by to pick it up as soon as you can; we will hold it for three weeks.

While you are in, you may want to browse around and see some of the other election-related titles we have recently received. New titles include:

- *Californians and the National Election* *$7.45*
- *The 1992 Election Year* *$19.95*
- *How Women Vote* *$9.95*

Present this letter for a 10% discount on any additional book you decide to buy in this category.

Yours sincerely,

Bill and Mary Lantern
Lantern Books

FIGURE 3.10:

The Create Envelope dialog box

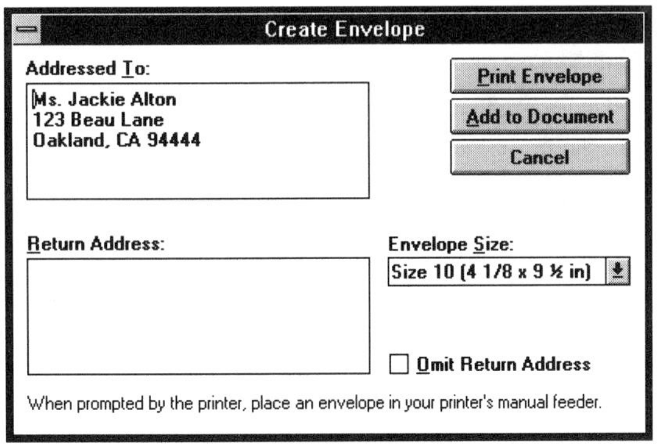

Create Envelope

Addressed To:
Ms. Jackie Alton
123 Beau Lane
Oakland, CA 94444

Print Envelope
Add to Document
Cancel

Return Address:

Envelope Size:
Size 10 (4 1/8 x 9 ½ in)

☐ Omit Return Address

When prompted by the printer, place an envelope in your printer's manual feeder.

SUMMARY

The ribbon and the ruler give you quick and convenient ways to improve the appearance of your document before you print it. On the ribbon you can choose fonts, point sizes, type styles, and alignments for the document. On the ruler you can change paragraph indents and margins. Using the ribbon and the ruler together, you can set new tab stops for selected lines in the document.

In addition, you have learned to use two important buttons on the Toolbar in this lesson: the Bulleted List button, which inserts bullets before each paragraph of a selection; and the Envelope button, which displays a dialog box where you can specify instructions for printing an envelope.

REFERENCE ENTRIES

For more information about formatting and printing a document, see the following entries in the reference section:

- *Formatting Text*
- *Formatting Paragraphs*
- *Formatting Pages*
- *Previewing*
- *Printing Envelopes*

PROOFING A DOCUMENT

Word has three important tools that will help you correct errors and improve your writing in the first draft of a document. You choose these three *proofing* commands from the Tools menu. The Spelling command finds misspelled words and suggests corrections. Clicking the Spelling button in the Toolbar is a shortcut for performing this command. The *Grammar* command checks for important categories of grammatical and stylistic flaws in your document, and suggests possible improvements. The *Thesaurus* provides lists of synonyms for words you select in your document.

In this lesson you'll type a document and then practice using Word's three proofing tools. The new document is an issue of a monthly newsletter published by the owners of Lantern Books. The first draft of the newsletter—complete with spelling errors—appears in Figures 4.1 and 4.2. This may seem like a lot of typing for one exercise, but you'll use this same document to learn about other Word features in *Lessons 5* and *6*.

TYPING THE NEWSLETTER

As you type this first draft, try to duplicate the spelling errors. Don't worry about any other typographical errors you might make as you enter the text. You'll use

FIGURE 4.1:

Page 1 of the newsletter, with spelling errors

Lantern Books
Newsletter
June 1992

Customers Settle into New Reading Area

As part of the current remodeling of our store, we are happy to announce the completion of a bright and comfortable new reading area, located between the reference section and the paperback fiction aisle. The area has two thick couches, several lamps, a rocking chair, and always a pot of hot coffee.

All our customers are invited to enjoy this area for quiet reading and reflexion:

- Look through a chapter of that new novel before you buy.
- Inspect a reference book to see if it's the one you need.
- Sit and read a story to your child.
- Spend a few minutes with this week's *New York Times Book Review,* a copy of which is always available for you to read in the store. (You'll also find copies of the *Book Review* for sale at the front cash register.)

The reading area is designed for our customers' enjoyment. Let us know if you think of any way we can improve it.

New Lantern Book Bags

Our Lantern-logo book bags are finally here! Colorful and attractive, these heavy-duty double-stitched canvas bags will hold half a dozen hard cover books, or a big load of paperbacks. Buy one for $2.95, or get one free with any purchase of $25.00 or more.

Lantern Books Features West African Writers in French

Perhaps because we are located near the French-American School, many of our regular customers are avid readers in French. In coordination with this month's West African film festival at the School, we're now featuring several African authors who write in French. You'll see their books displayed in the front of the foreign-language section. For example, you will find *Le mandat* and *Les bouts de bois de Dieu* by Ousmane Sembene.

As you may know, books from foreign publishers can be more expensive than books published in the United States. During the month of June we are offering a 10% discount on our entire library of foreign-language books.

Word's Spelling command to correct these errors. Follow these steps to create the newsletter; as you enter the text, be sure to save often:

1. Start Word for Windows; if the program is already running, click the New button to open a new empty document.

2. Save the document to disk as NEWSLETR.DOC.

3. Type the entire text of the newsletter first, without applying any specific formats or styles. Press ↵ twice after each main paragraph and after each heading, to insert blank lines. The document contains three lists; begin by typing them as individual lines or paragraphs of text without bullets, numbers, or indentations.

· FIGURE 4.2:

Page 2 of the newsletter, with spelling errors

In addition to French, we have selections of books in Cantonese, Dutch, German, Greek, Italian, Japanese, Russian, and Spanish. You'll also find dictionaries and other reference works for most of these languages.

Neighborhood Readers Forum Focusses on Election Books

The elections are upon us. We've stocked up on a variety of pertinent titles, including *Californians and the National Election* and *The 1992 Election Year Handbook.* You'll find these topical books displayed on the current-events table located near the front of the store.

This month's Neighborhood Readers Forum at the Lantern Bookstore (June 19 at 7:00 in the evening) will focus on these books and on the important issues of this year's election.

Calendar of Events
June 1992

- Wednesday, June 3 at noon *Children's story hour*
- Monday, June 15 at 3:00 p.m. *Local novelist Jane Hall will be here to sign copies of her new book,* Side Street
- Friday, June 19 at 7:00 p.m. *Neighborhood Readers Forum*
- Sunday, June 14 to Saturday, June 20 *African Film Festival at French-American School*
- Thursday, June 25 at 11:00 a.m. *Seniors' reading hour: readings and discussion of* Le Mandat, *the book and the movie*

Book Review in Brief:
Heart of San Francisco by Willa Madsen
224 pages, $19.95

This wry and wicked new novel takes place in the restarants, bars, streets, and neighborhoods of San Francisco. The protagonists, Jim and Mary Heart, are the smartest and funniest pair of fictional characters we've met in recent memory. Jim, an out-of-work lawyer, and Mary, an investigative journalist, together stumble onto a massive financial scandal that could rock the entire city and beyond. Be prepared for an earth-shaking conclusion.

Picks of the Month: The Staff's Favorites

1. *Home from the Moon,* by James Deller
2. *After Good-bye,* by Freida Maxton
3. *When in Paris,* by Ella Weinberg
4. *The New Russia,* by John Nelson
5. *Feeling Smart,* by Pat Tanner

4. Select the entire document and increase the point size to 12.

5. At the top of the document, center the first three lines. Change the first two lines to 18-point bold italics. Increase the point size of the third line—the date—to 14.

6. Select each of the seven headings in turn and change the font to 14-point Helvetica.

7. Select the book titles throughout the newsletter and click the Italics button for each one.

8. Select the list under the first heading of the newsletter and click the Bulleted List button to insert the bullets. Do the same for the list in the *Calendar of Events*. Then select the five lines in the last part of the newsletter (*Picks of the Month*) and click the Numbered List button—the eighth button in the Toolbar. Word inserts sequential numbers into the list and adjusts the indentation of each line.

You can use the Numbered List and Bulleted List buttons in either of two ways: Type the entire list first, then select the list and apply all the numbers or bullets at once (as you have done up to now); or, click the Numbered List or Bulleted List button once before each line as you type the list. To reset the starting number for a new numbered list, choose Tools ➤ Bullets and Numbering, click the Numbered List option button, and enter 1 (or any other starting number) into the Start At box. For more information, see **Bulleted Lists** *and* **Numbered Lists** *in* **Part II**.

CHECKING FOR MISSPELLED WORDS

You can check the spelling of an entire document in one efficient operation. But before you do so, you might want to identify certain portions of the text that should *not* be checked. For example, the newsletter contains two book titles in French, along with several authors' names that the Spelling command will not be able to recognize. The Language command in the Format menu allows you to establish passages such as these as text that Word should skip when proofing. Here are the steps:

1. Select the two French book titles and the author's name in the sentence that begins *For example, you will find* (in the first paragraph under the third heading).

2. Choose Format ➤ Language.

3. Scroll up to the top of the list labeled Mark Selected Text As. Choose the option identified as *(no proofing)*, as shown in Figure 4.3, and click OK.

4. Repeat this process for the authors' names and the French book title in the final three parts of the newsletter.

As you can see in Figure 4.3, the Language command also allows you to identify text that is written in a particular foreign language. In response, the Spelling command can search for each word in a designated foreign-language dictionary. But to make this feature work, you have to purchase each language dictionary separately and install it on your hard disk. (Microsoft supplies an order form for these dictionaries in the Word package.)

Now you are ready to check the spelling in the newsletter:

1. Press Ctrl-Home to move the insertion point to the beginning of the document.

2. Click the Spelling button, the fifth tool from the right on the Toolbar. In response, Word begins checking each word in the document, except for the special passages that you have identified. When the first misspelled word is found, the Spelling dialog box appears on the screen, as shown in Figure 4.4. The Not in Dictionary text box displays the word as it appears in the document, and the Change To box shows Word's suggestion for the correct spelling.

3. Click the Change button to replace the misspelled word with the correction. (Alternatively, if you think you might have misspelled the same word

FIGURE 4.3:

The Language dialog box

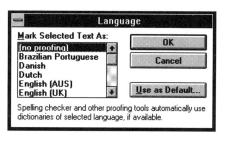

FIGURE 4.4:

The Spelling dialog box

additional times in the same document, click the Change All button to replace all instances.)

4. Continue clicking Change for each new misspelling that Word finds in your document. If your copy of the newsletter looks exactly like the document in Figures 4.1 and 4.2, Word finds the correct spellings for three words: *reflection*, *focuses*, and *restaurant*.

5. When Word finishes the spelling check, the dialog box shown in Figure 4.5 appears on the screen. Click OK to return to your document.

FIGURE 4.5:

The end of a
spelling check

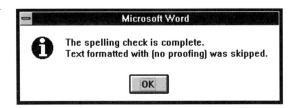

The Spelling command has no way of recognizing certain kinds of spelling errors. For example, Word will not find the error in the phrase **the paperback fiction isle**. The word **isle** is a correctly spelled word in English, even though it is incorrect in this context.

After you have checked the spelling, you should click the Save button to save the corrected document to disk.

To check the spelling of a single word, select the word and press F7. If the selected word is incorrect, the Spelling dialog box appears on the screen. If the word is correct, Word immediately tells you so and gives you the option of checking the rest of the document.

CHECKING THE GRAMMAR IN A DOCUMENT

The Tools ➤ Grammar command examines each sentence in your document and determines whether the text conforms to a collection of grammatical and stylistic rules. For each sentence that seems to break one or more of these rules, the Grammar dialog box displays the offending sentence along with a description of the potential problem.

Try using the Grammar command on the text of the newsletter:

1. Move the insertion point to the beginning of the document.

2. Choose Tools ➤ Grammar. The message *Word is checking the grammar in the document* appears on the status bar. After a few seconds, Word displays the first error in the Grammar dialog box, as shown in Figure 4.6. In this first example, Word has found a sentence in the passive voice.

3. To correct the sentence, click the mouse inside the text area in the letter. The sentence is highlighted in the document. Type this corrected version of the sentence:

   We invite you to use this area for quiet reading and reflection:

   Your new entry replaces the old sentence.

4. Click the Start button to resume the grammar check. The next sentence to appear in the Grammar box is also in the passive voice: *The reading area is designed for our customers' enjoyment.* Correct the sentence by clicking inside the text area and entering this new version:

   We have designed this area for your enjoyment.

5. Click Start again. Next the Grammar dialog box displays the sentence that begins *Perhaps because we are located.* Click the Ignore button to pass by this sentence without changing it.

6. The next sentence in the Grammar box is an incomplete sentence from the *Calendar of Events.* Click the Ignore Rule button to instruct Word to ignore this and other incomplete sentences it finds in the rest of the document.

Word has three levels of grammar checking: Strict, Business Writing, and Casual Writing. To change the level, click the Options button on the Grammar dialog box, and make a new selection in the resulting Options dialog box, shown in Figure 4.7.

FIGURE 4.6:

The Grammar dialog box

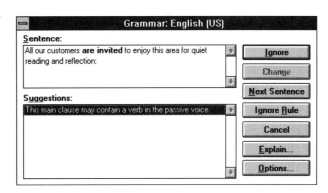

Furthermore, you can click the Customize Settings button (on the Options dialog box) to view and modify the lists of rules for a given level of checking.

When the grammar check is complete, Word displays a collection of statistics describing your document. The Readability Statistics dialog box shows the number of words, sentences, and paragraphs in your text, along with several standard measurements of the document's "readability," as shown in Figure 4.8. (Press F1 to bring up a Help screen that describes these statistics in detail.)

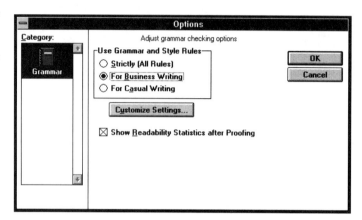

FIGURE 4.7:

The Options dialog box for the Grammar command

FIGURE 4.8:

The Readability Statistics dialog box

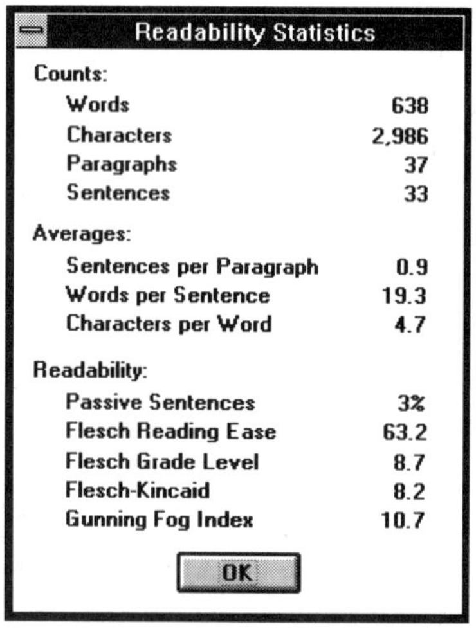

To view another set of statistics about your document, choose File ➤ Summary Info. Click the Statistics button on the Summary Info dialog box and the Document Statistics box appears on the screen. This dialog box tells you the number of words in your document, the number of times you have saved the document to disk, and the amount of time you have spent editing the document, along with other information.

USING THE THESAURUS

The Thesaurus is perhaps the most valuable of all Word's proofing tools. By offering you lists of synonymous or related words, the Thesaurus command helps you improve the precision, clarity, and style of your writing.

Use the Thesaurus whenever you would like to explore alternatives for a particular word in your document. First place the insertion point next to the target word, then choose Tools ➤ Thesaurus — or simply press Shift-F7 at the keyboard. For example, in the following exercise you'll locate the word *avid* in the newsletter, and you'll use the Thesaurus to replace the word with a synonym:

1. Move the insertion point to the top of the document.

2. Choose Edit ➤ Find. In the Find What text box, enter the word **avid,** then click the Find Next button. Word highlights *avid* in the first paragraph under the newsletter's third heading. Click the Cancel button to close the Find dialog box.

3. Press Shift-F7 to open the Thesaurus dialog box. Word presents the list of synonyms shown in Figure 4.9.

4. Select *enthusiastic* in the Synonyms list, then click the Replace button. In response, Word replaces *avid* with *enthusiastic* in the text of the newsletter.

5. Click the Save button to save the revised document to disk.

FIGURE 4.9:

The Thesaurus dialog box

*For some words the Thesaurus also presents a list of antonyms. See **Thesaurus** in **Part II** for more information.*

SUMMARY

The Spelling, Grammar, and Thesaurus commands are efficient tools for improving your writing in a Word document. Of course, each of these tools leaves the actual decisions to you: Only you can decide whether you want to make specific changes in your text. But Word's proofing tools can help you see possible weak points in your writing, and offer a variety of alternatives.

In *Lesson 5* you'll give the newsletter an entirely new look by organizing the text into a two-column format.

REFERENCE ENTRIES

See the following entries in *Part II* for more information:

- *Spelling Checks*
- *Grammar Checks*
- *Thesaurus*

LESSON FIVE

REORGANIZING A DOCUMENT

Word gives you detailed control over the way your document will appear on the printed page. For example, in this lesson you will transform your copy of the Lantern Books newsletter into the document you see in Figures 5.1 and 5.2. As you can see, this reformatted newsletter illustrates several new visual and organizational features, all of which you will learn about in this lesson.

◆ A *footer* is text that appears at the bottom of each page of a document. (Likewise, a *header* is text at the top of each page.) The newsletter's footer displays the name of the bookstore, the date, and the page number.

◆ A *section* is a portion of a document that has its own formatting characteristics. In the revised newsletter, there are two sections: The banner at the top of page 1 is the first section and the remainder of the text is the second.

◆ *Newspaper-style columns* are parallel columns of text. (Word also allows you to create *table columns*, which you'll learn about in *Lesson 7*.)

FIGURE 5.1:

The reorganized newsletter, page 1

Lantern Books Newsletter
June 1992

Customers Settle into New Reading Area

As part of the current remodeling of our store, we are happy to announce the completion of a bright and comfortable new reading area, located between the reference section and the paperback fiction aisle. The area has two thick couches, several lamps, a rocking chair, and always a pot of hot coffee.

We invite you to use this area for quiet reading and reflection:

New Lantern Book Bags

Our Lantern-logo book bags are finally here! Colorful and attractive, these heavy-duty double-stitched canvas bags will hold half a dozen hard cover books, or a big load of paperbacks. Buy one for $2.95, or get one free with any purchase of $25.00 or more.

- Look through a chapter of that new novel before you buy.
- Inspect a reference book to see if it's the one you need.
- Sit and read a story to your child.
- Spend a few minutes with this week's *New York Times Book Review*, a copy of which is always available for you to read in the store. (You'll also find copies of the *Book Review* for sale at the front cash register.)

We have designed this area for your enjoyment. Let us know if you think of any way we can improve it.

Lantern Books Features West African Writers in French

Perhaps because we are located near the French-American School, many of our regular customers are enthusiastic readers in French.

In coordination with this month's West African film festival at the School, we're now featuring several African authors who write in French. You'll see their books displayed in the front of the foreign-language section. For example, you will find *Le mandat* and *Les bouts de bois de Dieu* by Ousmane Sembene.

As you may know, books from foreign publishers can be more expensive than books published in the United States. During the month of June we are offering a 10% discount on our entire library of foreign-language books.

In addition to French, we have selections of books in Cantonese, Dutch, German, Greek, Italian, Japanese, Russian, and Spanish.

You'll also find dictionaries and other reference works for most of these languages.

FIGURE 5.2:
The reorganized newsletter, page 2

Neighborhood Readers Forum Focuses on Election Books

The elections are upon us. We've stocked up on a variety of pertinent titles, including *Californians and the National Election* and *The 1992 Election Year Handbook*. You'll find these topical books displayed on the current-events table located near the front of the store.

This month's Neighborhood Readers Forum at the Lantern Bookstore (June 19 at 7:00 in the evening) will focus on these books and on the important issues of this year's election.

Calendar of Events
June 1992

- Wednesday, June 3 at noon *Children's story hour*
- Monday, June 15 at 3:00 p.m. *Local novelist Jane Hall will be here to sign copies of her new book,* Side Street
- Friday, June 19 at 7:00 p.m. *Neighborhood Readers Forum*
- Sunday, June 14 to Saturday, June 20 *African Film Festival at French-American School*

- Thursday, June 25 at 11:00 a.m. *Seniors' reading hour: readings and discussion of* Le Mandat, *the book and the movie*

Book Review in Brief:
Heart of San Francisco
by Willa Madsen
224 pages, $19.95

This wry and wicked new novel takes place in the restaurants, bars, streets, and neighborhoods of San Francisco. The protagonists, Jim and Mary Heart, are the smartest and funniest pair of fictional characters we've met in recent memory. Jim, an out-of-work lawyer, and Mary, an investigative journalist, together stumble onto a massive financial scandal that could rock the entire city and beyond. Be prepared for an earth-shaking conclusion.

Picks of the Month: The Staff's Favorites

1. *Home from the Moon,* by James Deller
2. *After Good-bye*, by Freida Maxton
3. *When in Paris*, by Ella Weinberg
4. *The New Russia*, by John Nelson
5. *Feeling Smart*, by Pat Tanner

- A *frame* is a moveable portion of text. The ad for book bags is located in a frame near the center of the newsletter's first page. Notice how the two columns of text wrap around the frame.

- A *border* is a box surrounding a block of text. You can see borders around three blocks of text in the newsletter—the banner at the top of page 1, the frame of text in the center of the page, and the footer at the bottom of each page.

Although these may seem like elaborate changes, you'll be able to accomplish them all in just a few minutes after a little practice. To get ready for the work ahead of you, begin now by opening NEWSLETR.DOC if it is not already open.

As you work through this lesson, you may find that the document you produce on your screen does not exactly match the newsletter as it is shown in Figures 5.1 and 5.2. When you add sections, columns, and frames to the document, the outcome depends on the characteristics of the font you are using. If you do get different results, use this opportunity to experiment with the newsletter to produce a format that appeals to your own sense of aesthetics.

ADDING A FOOTER TO THE DOCUMENT

To add a header or a footer to a document, you choose View ➤ Header/Footer. As you can see in the Header/Footer dialog box, shown in Figure 5.3, this command gives you several important options—including the ability to create distinct headers and footers for odd and even pages, and for the document's first page. For the newsletter, however, you'll design a uniform footer for the entire document.

Throughout most of this lesson you'll be working in Page Layout view, but headers and footers are easier to create in Normal view:

1. Choose View ➤ Normal.

2. Choose View ➤ Header/Footer. In the Header/Footer box, select the Footer option and then click the OK button. In response, Word opens a *footer pane* at the bottom of the text area, as shown in Figure 5.4. Notice the elements of the bar at the top of the new pane. In particular, note the three buttons at the beginning of the bar for adding the page number, the date, and the time to your footer.

3. Click the Center and Bold buttons on the ribbon. Type **Lantern Books**. Then click the Bold button to toggle back into normal type. Press the Spacebar five times. Type **Newsletter** and then press the Spacebar five more times. Click the Italics button on the ribbon and type **June 1992**.

FIGURE 5.3:

The Header/Footer dialog box

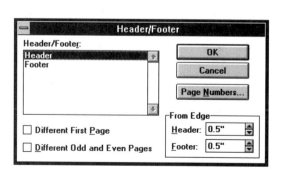

Click the Italics button again to return to normal type. Press the Spacebar five times and type the word **Page** followed by one space. Finally, click the Page Number button at the beginning of the header/footer bar. The current page number, 1, appears in the footer text.

4. Choose Format ➤ Border. The Border Paragraphs dialog box appears on the screen, as shown in Figure 5.5. In the Line box, select the thin double-line border style, just below the None option. Click OK. A double-line border appears around the text of the footer.

5. Click the Close button on the header/footer bar.

FIGURE 5.4:

The header/footer pane

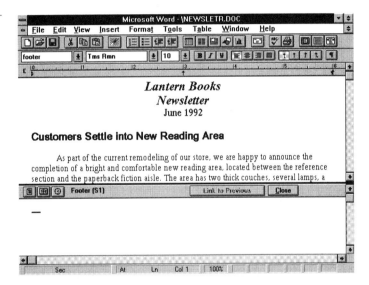

FIGURE 5.5:

The Border Paragraphs dialog box

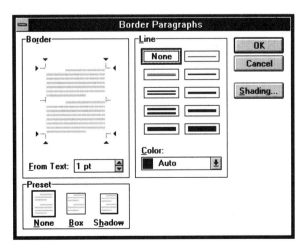

> *The header/footer pane is available only in Normal view, but a document's headers and footers are displayed only in Page Layout view. For more information, see **Headers and Footers** in **Part II**. Also, see **Borders**.*

Now use the Border command again to create a banner at the top of the newsletter:

1. Select the first three lines of the document, and then choose Format ➤ Border.

2. Select the thin double-line border in the Line box. Then click the Shadow option in the Preset box. Click OK.

CREATING SECTIONS AND COLUMNS

The next step is to divide the document into two sections. The first section is the three-line banner, which is already in its final format. The second section is the remainder of the text, which you will organize into the two newspaper-style columns. The section break allows you to apply these two different formats to portions of the document:

1. Move the insertion point to the beginning of the line that contains the heading *Customers Settle into New Reading Area.*

2. Choose Insert ➤ Break. In the Break dialog box, select the Continuous option, as shown in Figure 5.6. This option creates a section break without starting a new page. Click OK. A dotted double line indicates the section break in the document.

3. Choose View ➤ Page Layout. In Page Layout view the section break is no longer displayed, but it is still there. (When the insertion point is inside the second section, the notation *Sec 2* appears on the status bar.)

4. Without moving the insertion point, click the Text Columns button, the thirteenth button on the Toolbar. A column grid drops down from the button, as you can see in Figure 5.7. Click the mouse over the second column

FIGURE 5.6:

The Break dialog box

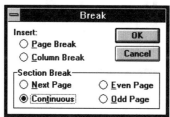

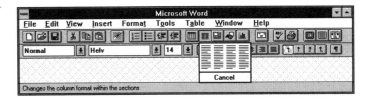

in the grid. The words *2 columns* appear beneath the grid. When you release the mouse button, Word reorganizes the text of section 2 into two newspaper-style columns. Scrolling down the document, you'll see that the two-column format has been applied to both pages.

5. With the insertion point still inside section 2, choose Format ➤ Columns. In the Columns dialog box, select the Line Between option. (An X appears in the option box.) Click OK. The line between the two columns does not show up in the text area, but you will see it when you print your document.

CREATING AND MOVING A FRAME

Now you're ready to define a frame for the text of the book-bag ad. Once you've created the frame, you can move it anywhere in your document in Page Layout view. Word will arrange other text around the frame.

Although a frame can have its own border, there is an important distinction in Word between a border and a frame. A border is simply a visual effect—a way of setting off a block of text by enclosing it in a box. A frame is a moveable block of text.

Here are the steps for creating and moving the frame in the newsletter:

1. Move the insertion point to the blank line just above the heading *New Lantern Book Bags*. Use the keyboard or the mouse to select the heading and the entire paragraph that goes with it, plus the blank lines above the heading and below the paragraph. (If the paragraph is initially broken across the columns, you may find it easier to use the keyboard to make this selection: Hold down Shift and press ↓ and → until the entire selection is highlighted.)

2. Click the Frame button, located just to the right of the Text Columns button on the Toolbar. Word encloses the selection in a single-line border with handles. This block is now a frame.

3. Move the mouse pointer over any part of the frame's border. The pointer becomes a four-headed arrow icon. Drag the frame toward its new location, as shown in Figure 5.1. A shadow of the frame moves along with the mouse pointer. Position the upper line of the shadow just beneath the bottom line of the first paragraph of the text and center the frame horizontally. Release the mouse button. Word moves the frame to its new position and rearranges the two columns of text around it.

4. While the frame is still selected, choose Format ➤ Frame. The Frame dialog box has two different text boxes labeled Distance from Text, for adjusting the horizontal and vertical orientation of the frame. Enter **.25** (representing ¼″) into each of these text boxes and click OK. This increases the amount of blank space between the frame and the surrounding text.

5. With the frame still selected, choose Format ➤ Border. Click the second single-line frame option in the Line box and then click the Shadow option in the Preset box. Finish up by clicking OK.

WARNING

*While the frame is selected, be careful not to press Del inadvertently. Doing so will delete the entire frame and its text contents. (If you accidently press Del, immediately click the Undo button.) See the **Frames** entry in **Part II** for more information.*

The newsletter is almost in its final form now. After making a few minor adjustments, you'll be ready to print it.

ADJUSTING THE COLUMNS AND THE MARGINS

One of the difficulties in the layout of a multi-column document is creating uniform-length columns on each page. You may have to experiment to achieve the effect you want. Sometimes you can adjust the length of a column manually by revising the text itself or by inserting column breaks. But you can also use a special Word feature to create columns that are equal in length: If you insert a section break at the bottom of a page of columns, Word adjusts the column lengths for you. You'll try these techniques in the following steps, and then you'll use Page Preview to adjust margins before you print the document:

1. On the first page, insert two new paragraph breaks into the text: Position the insertion point just before the sentence that begins *In coordination with* in the first paragraph under the second heading; press ↵ twice, and press

Tab. Then position the insertion point before the sentence *You'll also find dictionaries* in the final paragraph under the same heading; press ⏎ twice and then Tab.

2. If the headings *Lantern Books Features...* and *Neighborhood Readers Forum...* do not already appear at the tops of their columns (as in Figures 5.1 and 5.2), move the insertion point to the beginning of each heading in turn, choose Insert ➤ Break, click the Column Break option, and click OK. After you make these changes, you'll have to reposition the frame for the book-bag ad.

3. Press Ctrl-End to move the insertion point to the end of the document—that is, at the end of the right-hand column on the second page.

4. Choose Insert ➤ Break. Click the Continuous option and then click OK to insert a section break at this position in the text. As a result, Word automatically adjusts the lengths of the two columns on the second page.

5. Press Ctrl-Home to move to the beginning of the document. Then choose File ➤ Print Preview. If only one page appears in the Preview window, click the Two Pages button.

6. Click the Margin button and then click on the second page of text. The margin lines appear in the second page. Drag the top margin line down to about the 2″ level. Then click the Margin button again. The two columns are now approximately centered vertically on the second page, as shown in Figure 5.8.

7. Click the Print button if you want to print the document. Click OK on the Print dialog box.

FIGURE 5.8:

The two pages of the newsletter in the Preview window

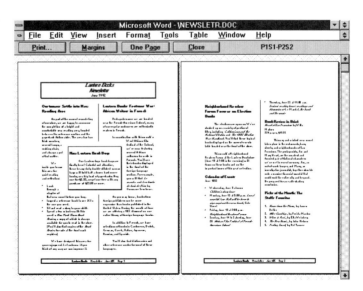

8. Click the Close button in the Preview window, then click the Save button on the Toolbar to save your work to disk.

SUMMARY

You can use sections, columns, frames, and borders to create a variety of visual and organizational effects in a Word document. Dividing your document into sections allows you to apply different formats to different parts of the text. Creating columns and frames are essentially one-click operations thanks to the buttons available for these features in the Toolbar.

In *Lesson 6* you'll continue your work with the Lantern Books newsletter, adding some graphics to the document.

REFERENCE ENTRIES

See the following entries for more information about organizing a document:

- *Headers and Footers*
- *Columns*
- *Frames*
- *Sections*
- *Borders*

ADDING WORDART
AND PICTURES

INTRODUCING

The WordArt Program
Microsoft Draw
*Copying a Graphic
to Another File*

You can incorporate pictures and graphics from other programs to enhance a Word for Windows document. In fact, Word comes with a collection of easy but effective programs with which you can create graphics. *Microsoft WordArt* is a program you can use to produce special typographical effects for a document. *Microsoft Draw* is a drawing program in which you can create icons, logos, and other pictorial objects. *Microsoft Graph* produces several kinds of charts and graphs from tables of numeric data.

In this lesson you'll experiment with WordArt and Draw as you add a simple logo to the end of the Lantern Books newsletter. (In *Lesson 7*, you'll turn your attention to the features of the Graph program.) Figure 6.1 shows how page 2 of the newsletter will appear when you complete this lesson's exercises.

FIGURE 6.1:

The newsletter with a logo

Neighborhood Readers Forum Focuses on Election Books

The elections are upon us. We've stocked up on a variety of pertinent titles, including *Californians and the National Election* and *The 1992 Election Year Handbook*. You'll find these topical books displayed on the current-events table located near the front of the store.

This month's Neighborhood Readers Forum at the Lantern Bookstore (June 19 at 7:00 in the evening) will focus on these books and on the important issues of this year's election.

Calendar of Events
June 1992

- Wednesday, June 3 at noon *Children's story hour*
- Monday, June 15 at 3:00 p.m. *Local novelist Jane Hall will be here to sign copies of her new book,* Side Street
- Friday, June 19 at 7:00 p.m. *Neighborhood Readers Forum*
- Sunday, June 14 to Saturday, June 20 *African Film Festival at French-American School*
- Thursday, June 25 at 11:00 a.m. *Seniors' reading hour: readings and discussion of* Le Mandat, *the book and the movie*

Book Review in Brief:
Heart of San Francisco
by Willa Madsen
224 pages, $19.95

This wry and wicked new novel takes place in the restaurants, bars, streets, and neighborhoods of San Francisco. The protagonists, Jim and Mary Heart, are the smartest and funniest pair of fictional characters we've met in recent memory. Jim, an out-of-work lawyer, and Mary, an investigative journalist, together stumble onto a massive financial scandal that could rock the entire city and beyond. Be prepared for an earth-shaking conclusion.

Picks of the Month: The Staff's Favorites

1. *Home from the Moon,* by James Deller
2. *After Good-bye*, by Freida Maxton
3. *When in Paris*, by Ella Weinberg
4. *The New Russia*, by John Nelson
5. *Feeling Smart,* by Pat Tanner

9898 Santa Barbara Avenue
San Francisco, CA 94000

(415) 555-9999

Lantern Books Newsletter *June 1992* Page 2

Graphics that you transfer into a document from the WordArt, Draw, or Graph programs are known as embedded objects. (The Microsoft Equation Editor is a fourth program that is included with Word to create embedded objects. The Equation Editor is useful for preparing complex mathematical equations in technical documents.) You can start any of these programs by choosing Insert ➤ Object and selecting a name from the list that appears in the Object dialog box. Alternatively, you can start the Draw program or the Graph program by clicking the corresponding button on the Toolbar.

USING MICROSOFT WORDART

When you start WordArt, the window shown in Figure 6.2 appears over the Word window. Creating special typographical effects is simple: You begin by typing one or more lines into the text box at the upper-left corner of the WordArt window. Then you select options for the text from the Font, Size, Style, Fill, and Align boxes and from the Options frame. As you enter and modify the text, the WordArt object you are creating appears in the Preview box. When you have created exactly the effect you want, click OK to transfer the object to your current document at the insertion point.

Here are the steps for creating the WordArt object you saw back in Figure 6.1:

1. Open the NEWSLETR.DOC file, and press Ctrl-End to move the insertion point to the end of the document. Choose View ➤ Normal so you can see the double line representing the section break at the end of the file. Press the Backspace key one time to delete the break. Then choose View ➤ Page Layout. Page 2 of the document returns to its original format, with the default top margin setting and the uneven column lengths.

FIGURE 6.2:

The WordArt window

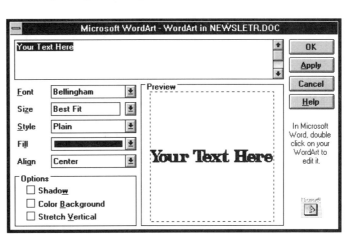

The formatting instructions for a section are contained in the section break; when you delete the break, you also delete the formatting.

2. Press ⏎ three times, and then click the Center button on the ribbon.

3. Choose Insert ➤ Object. In the Object Type list, choose MS WordArt, and then click OK. After a few seconds the Microsoft WordArt window appears.

4. Type **Lantern Books** into the text box at the top of the window. (Your typing replaces the highlighted text initially in the window.)

5. Pull down the Font list and choose the font named Sequim.

6. Pull down the Style list and choose the Arch Up option. At this point, your WordArt text appears as in Figure 6.3.

7. Click OK to transfer this text to NEWSLETR.DOC. When you return to the document, the insertion point appears immediately after the WordArt object. Press ⏎ once.

By selecting options in the Style list of the WordArt window, you can achieve a variety of amusing typographical effects—including slanted, rounded, arched, vertical, and upside-down text. To edit a WordArt object already embedded in a document, you simply double-click the object. In response, Word restarts WordArt and places the object back in the program's text box. (In fact, you can double-click any embedded object to start up the program in which the object was originally created.)

FIGURE 6.3:

Creating a
WordArt object

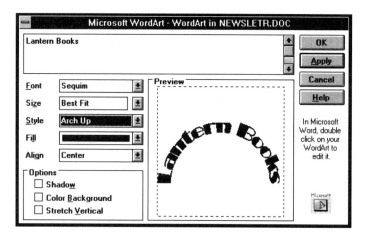

USING MICROSOFT DRAW

When you click the Draw button (located just to the right of the Frame button on the Toolbar), the Microsoft Draw window opens onto the screen, as shown in Figure 6.4. At the left side of the window is a collection of tools that you can use to draw objects in the work area—including lines, circles, ellipses, squares, rectangles, wedges, freehand drawings, and text. At the bottom of the window are two rows of colors from which you select the drawing color and the fill color. In addition, Draw's menus offer a variety of other options that change the appearance of the objects you draw.

Even a user who has no artistic ability can use Draw to create effective pictures for use in Word documents. For example, the newsletter's book logo, shown back in Figure 6.1, is simply a row of rectangles filled with black, white, and shades of gray. Here are the steps for creating this logo and adding it to the newsletter document:

1. Click the Draw button on the Toolbar. After a few seconds, the Microsoft Draw window appears on the screen.

2. Click the rectangle drawing tool at the left side of the window. On the Fill line at the bottom of the window, click the dark gray square, the fourth color from the left.

3. Move the mouse pointer into the work area. The pointer appears in a crosshair shape. Drag the pointer into the shape of the first rectangle, and then release the mouse button. As shown in Figure 6.5, the Draw program fills the resulting rectangle with the dark gray color you have selected on the Fill line.

4. Click elsewhere in the work area to deselect the first rectangle. Then repeat steps 2 and 3 to create each of the next four rectangles. Select fill

FIGURE 6.4:

The Draw window

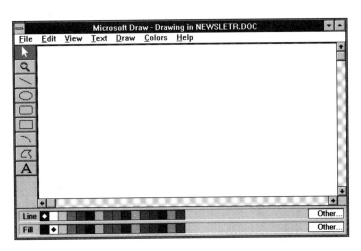

colors of light gray, black, white, and light gray again. Start each new rectangle at the lower-right corner of the previous rectangle, and try to match the heights and widths of the rectangles shown in Figure 6.5.

5. Choose Draw's File ➤ Exit and Return to NEWSLETR.DOC command.

6. A dialog box appears on the screen with the question *Update NEWSLETR.DOC?* Click the Yes button in this box. As a result, the book logo that you have just drawn appears in the newsletter, just beneath the arched text.

7. Press ↵ twice. Change the font to 14-point Helvetica, and type the bookstore's address and phone number, as shown back in Figure 6.1.

8. If the columns on page 2 are not even in length, choose Insert ➤ Break to insert a section break after the phone number.

9. Click the Save button to save your work to disk, and then click the Print button to print a copy of the newsletter.

You might see the following notation in the place where you were expecting to find the logo you've drawn:

{EMBED MSDraw * mergeformat}

These are the field codes for the embedded Draw object. If this is what you see, choose View ➤ Field Codes to view the drawing itself. For more information, see **Fields** *in* **Part II** *of this book.*

FIGURE 6.5:

Creating a picture

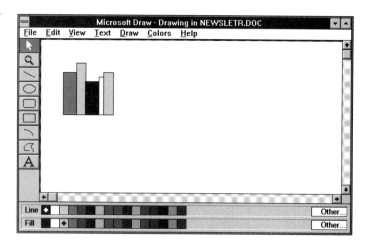

COPYING THE
BOOK LOGO TO ANOTHER FILE

Now that you have created a logo, you might want to copy it to other documents. In the this lesson's final exercise, you'll copy the book logo to the letter that you completed in *Lesson 3*:

1. In the newsletter document, click the mouse once over the book drawing you have just created. Handles appear around the drawing, indicating that the object is selected.

2. Click the Copy button on the Toolbar (or choose Edit ➤ Copy). This copies the object to the Windows Clipboard.

3. Choose File ➤ Open and open the BOOKLETR.DOC file.

4. Select the top five lines of the document—those containing the return address and the date. Click the Left-Align button on the ribbon to move the text in these lines back to the left border.

5. Select the first line and click the Underline button to remove the underlining from the name of the bookstore.

6. Move the insertion point to the beginning of the document, just to the left of the *L* in *Lantern Books*.

7. Click the Paste button in the Toolbar (or choose Edit ➤ Paste). In response, Word copies the book logo to the letter, producing the effect shown in Figure 6.6.

8. Click the Save button to save the new version of the letter to disk, then click the Print button to print a copy of the letter.

---

*You now have two documents open at once: one called NEWSLETR.DOC and another called BOOKLETR.DOC. Word allows you to open multiple files so that you can easily perform operations such as copy-and-paste across documents. Pull down the Window menu to see a list of all the documents that are open at a given time. To view an open document, choose the document's file name from the Window menu. For more information, see **Window Arrangements** in **Part II.***

FIGURE 6.6:

A logo for the
bookstore letterhead

Lantern Books
9898 Santa Barbara Avenue
San Francisco, CA 94000

2 June 1992

Ms. Jackie Alton
123 Beau Lane
Oakland, CA 94444

Dear Ms. Alton:

We are happy to let you know that the book you ordered, ***Electing the American President***, has arrived from the publisher. The price of the book is $21.95. Stop by to pick it up as soon as you can; we will hold it for three weeks.

While you are in, you may want to browse around and see some of the other election-related titles we have recently received. New titles include:

- *Californians and the National Election*   *$7.45*
- *The 1992 Election Year*   *$19.95*
- *How Women Vote*   *$9.95*

Present this letter for a 10% discount on any additional book you decide to buy in this category.

Yours sincerely,

Bill and Mary Lantern
Lantern Books

SUMMARY

Word for Windows comes with a collection of versatile programs that produce embedded objects in your current document: WordArt, Draw, Equation Editor, and Graph. All of these programs are easy to use, and fun to work with. In *Lesson 7* you'll try your hand at creating some charts with the Graph program.

REFERENCE ENTRIES

See the following entries in *Part II* for more information about the WordArt and Draw programs:

- *WordArt*
- *Draw*

CREATING TABLES AND CHARTS

A *table* in Word is an arrangement of data in rows and columns. The intersection of a row and a column is called a *cell*. In the cells of a table you can enter numbers, labels, multi-line blocks of text, or even embedded graphic objects. For multiple rows and columns of information, a table is often easier to manage than a set of tab stops. What's more, you can quickly create a chart or graph from any table of numbers and labels.

As you learn to create tables and charts in this lesson, you'll produce the sample document shown in Figure 7.1, an in-house memo to the staff of Lantern Books. The table of numeric data in the memo shows the average number of sales in the store during the six days of the business week and during different hours of the day. Once you have created this table, you'll use Microsoft Graph to create the two charts that also appear in the document: a column chart illustrating the average daily sales levels and a pie chart showing the customer traffic during the hours of a typical business day.

To prepare for this lesson, begin by entering the memo's heading and the three paragraphs of text into a blank document. (Copy the bookstore's logo and name from the BOOKLETR.DOC file.) Format the text in 12-point Times Roman and enter two blank lines between the paragraphs at the positions where you'll create the table and the charts. Save the document to disk as BOOKMEMO.DOC.

· FIGURE 7.1:

· A table and
· two charts

Lantern Books

Memorandum
To: Part-time sales staff
From: Mary Lantern
RE: Summer work schedules

Last summer we tracked the frequency of individual sales during the days of the business week and during the hours of each day. From this data I have calculated the following average daily sales frequencies:

	Morning	Afternoon	Evening
Mon.	3	9	15
Tues.	7	22	29
Wed.	6	17	25
Thurs.	14	38	42
Fri.	21	33	36
Sat.	25	59	49
TOTAL	76	178	196

If the coming summer matches last summer's patterns, we can expect to have more business on Thursdays, Fridays, and Saturdays than on the first three days of the week. Our busiest times during most days are evenings and afternoons:

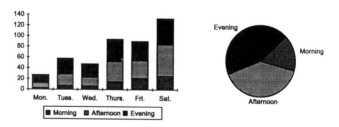

As I plan the summer's work schedules, I am doing my best to meet your individual preferences, but I appreciate your willingness to be flexible.

CREATING A TABLE

In planning a table, you first decide how many rows and columns of information the table will initially contain. Then you use the Table button on the Toolbar to create the table. Word displays the new table as an empty grid of cells, bordered by dotted lines. You can then begin applying formats to selected rows and columns and entering data into the cells of the table.

*After you have created a table you can change its dimensions by selecting rows or columns and choosing the Insert Rows, Insert Columns, Delete Rows, or Delete Columns commands in the Table menu. See the **Tables** entry in **Part II** for more information.*

Follow these steps to create the table in the bookstore memo:

1. Move the insertion point to the blank line just above the document's second paragraph.

2. Click the Table button (the twelfth button on the Toolbar). A grid of cells drops down beneath the button. Drag the mouse pointer across and down this grid until you see the notation *8 x 4 Table* on the line beneath the grid, as shown in Figure 7.2. Release the mouse button and Word inserts the new empty table into your document. The insertion point is inside the first cell of the table.

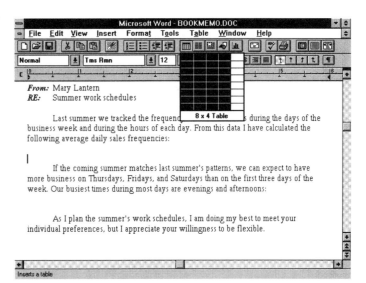

3. Hold down the Alt key and press the 5 key on the number pad. (The Num Lock key must be toggled off.) This action selects the entire table.

4. Choose Table ➤ Column Width. In the Column Width dialog box, the text box labeled Width of Columns shows the default width of each column in the new table as 1.5″. Enter a new value of **1** into this box and click OK to decrease the column width of the entire table.

5. Notice that the ruler now displays the *table scale*, in which each column width is marked by a bold **T**. Drag the first column marker left to the ¾″ line, slightly decreasing the width of the table's first column. Then drag the left-indent marker right to the ½″ line; this moves the entire table to the right.

6. Position the mouse pointer in the selection bar, just to the left of the table's first row. (As usual, the mouse pointer becomes a white arrow pointing up and to the right.) Click the left mouse button to select the entire first row. Then click the Bold button on the ribbon. Repeat these same two steps on the bottom row of the table. The information you later type into these two rows will be displayed in bold.

7. Position the mouse pointer just above the first column; the pointer takes the shape of a black arrow pointing down. Click the left mouse button to select the entire first column, then click the Bold button on the ribbon.

8. Position the mouse pointer above the second column. When you see the down-pointing black arrow, drag the mouse to the right, selecting the second, third, and fourth columns of the table. Click the Right-align button on the ribbon. As a result, the data in these columns will be right-aligned within each cell.

9. Click inside the second cell of the first row, and enter the word **Morning**. Press the Tab key to move the insertion point to the next cell in the table. Continue entering the remaining labels and numbers into the table, as shown in Figure 7.3. (If you make a mistake in an entry, press Shift-Tab to select the previous cell in the table and retype the entry.) For now, leave the last three cells in the bottom row blank.

At the left side of each cell is an individual selection bar, just like the one at the left side of a document. You can click inside a cell's selection bar to highlight the entire cell.

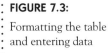

FIGURE 7.3:

Formatting the table and entering data

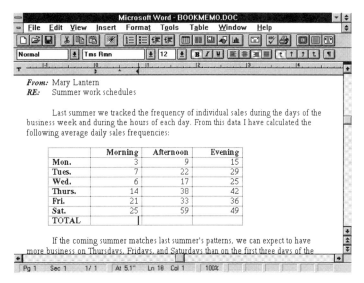

PERFORMING CALCULATIONS IN A TABLE

You can use Tools ➤ Calculate to perform simple arithmetic calculations in a table. By default this command finds the sum of all the numbers in a selection and stores the result in the Clipboard. For example, here are the steps for finding the totals in the bottom row of your table:

1. Click above the table's second column to select the entire column.

2. Choose Tools ➤ Calculate. Word displays the following message in the status bar: *The result of the calculation is: 76.*

3. Click inside the bottom cell in the second column. Then click the Paste button in the Toolbar (or choose Edit ➤ Paste). Word pastes the result, 76, into the cell.

4. Repeat these steps to insert totals into the bottom cells of the table's third and fourth columns. (The totals for these columns are 178 and 196.)

5. Click the Save button to save your work to disk.

*To perform specific arithmetic calculations, include arithmetic operators (+, −, *, /, ^) along with numeric values in an expression anywhere in a document. Highlight the expression and choose the Calculate command to find the solution. See **Calculations** in **Part II** for more information.*

CREATING CHARTS FROM A TABLE

The Microsoft Graph program creates charts and graphs that you can add to a document as embedded objects. The simplest way to create a chart is to select all or part of the data in a table and then click the Graph button in the Toolbar. In response, Word copies the selected table data to the Graph program. In the following exercise, you'll produce a column chart from the top seven rows of data in the table you've created:

1. Move the mouse pointer into the selection bar just to the left of the first row in the table. Drag the pointer down to the second-to-last row to select the table's first seven rows. (The total row is not needed for this first chart.)

2. Click the Graph button, located between the Draw and Envelope buttons on the Toolbar. After a few seconds, the Microsoft Graph window opens over the Word window. Click the maximize button at the upper-right corner of the Graph window. The application displays a Datasheet containing the data from your table and a Chart window that displays a column chart initially created from the data.

3. Rearrange the application window as you see it in Figure 7.4: Drag the Chart window toward the lower-right corner of the screen, and enlarge the Datasheet window by dragging its bottom border down.

4. Choose Data Series ➤ Series in Columns. In response, the Graph program redraws the column chart so that the days of the week appear along the horizontal axis and the labels *Morning*, *Afternoon*, and *Evening* appear in the legend.

FIGURE 7.4:

The Graph window

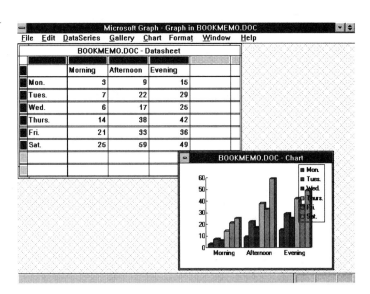

5. Choose Gallery ➤ Column. In the Chart Gallery dialog box, choose the third column chart option, as shown in Figure 7.5. Click OK and the program again redraws the chart, now producing a stacked-column chart.

6. In the Chart window, click inside the chart's legend. Handles appear around the perimeter of the legend. Next choose Format ➤ Legend. In the Legend dialog box, click the Bottom option and click OK. In response, the Graph program moves the legend beneath the chart.

7. Choose File ➤ Exit and Return to BOOKMEMO.DOC. A dialog box appears with the prompt *Update Graph in BOOKMEMO.DOC?* Click the Yes button. The Graph program copies the column chart to your document as an embedded object. Initially the chart appears immediately beneath the table from which it was created.

8. Click the chart once to select it. Then drag it to its correct position between the second and third paragraphs of the memo.

CREATING A PIE CHART

The pie chart in the memo is based on only two rows of data: The table's top row, containing labels, and the bottom row, containing totals. To create this chart, you'll copy the entire table to the Graph program, but then you'll instruct the program to use only the first and last rows to produce the chart. Here are the steps:

1. Move the insertion point to any cell in the table, and press Alt-5 (number pad) to select the entire table.

2. Click the Graph button. When the Graph application window appears, click the maximize button and rearrange the Datasheet and Chart windows as in the previous exercise.

3. In the Datasheet window, notice the column of small black squares located just to the left of the first column of data. These are called the row headings. Drag the mouse pointer down the row headings for the second

FIGURE 7.5:

The Chart Gallery dialog box

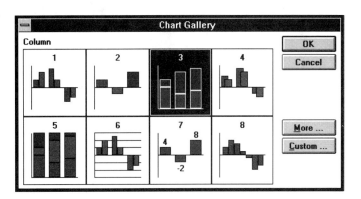

through seventh rows in the table—that is, the rows labeled *Mon.* through *Sat.* In response, the Graph program highlights the six rows.

4. Choose DataSeries ➤ Exclude Row/Col. The Graph program redraws the default column chart to represent only the two remaining rows—the first and the last, as shown in Figure 7.6.

5. Choose Gallery ➤ Pie. Select the fifth pie chart option and click OK.

6. In the Chart window, click the legend to select it. Then press Del to delete the legend from the chart.

7. Choose File ➤ Exit and Return to BOOKMEMO.DOC. Click Yes in response to *Update Graph in BOOKMEMO.DOC?* The new pie chart appears in the BOOKMEMO.DOC document.

8. Select the new chart and drag it to its correct position to the right of the column chart. (Resize the chart object, if necessary.) Your document now looks like Figure 7.1.

9. Click the Save button, then click the Print button if you want to print a copy of the document.

SUMMARY

A table is a convenient tool for entering and formatting data in a Word document. Given a table of numeric data and labels, you can use the versatile Graph program to create charts and graphs for a document.

FIGURE 7.6:

Excluding rows from the chart

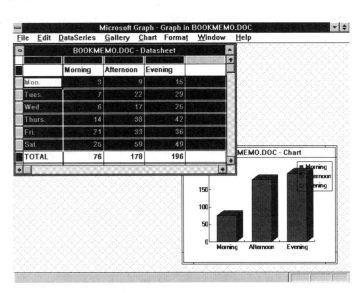

Tables have many additional uses in Word. For example, you can use a table to create a database for a print-merge operation. You'll learn about this feature in *Lesson 8*.

REFERENCE ENTRIES

For more information see the following entries in *Part II*:

Tables

Graph

USING THE
PRINT MERGE FEATURE

With Word's *print merge* feature you can automate the production of personalized form letters. The idea is simple: You compose a single business letter to send to many different people—for example, a specific list of customers—but you want each printed copy of the letter to appear unique and personal. Rather than the uninspiring *Dear Sir or Madame*, you want the letters to read *Dear Ms. Alton, Dear Mr. Johnston, Dear Dr. Smith*, and so on. You also want other parts of each letter to contain information that is relevant to an individual customer.

To carry out a print merge, you create two separate document files:

♦ A main document containing the basic text that you want to include in every copy of the letter. For example, in this lesson you'll revise the BOOKLETR.DOC file to create a main document for a print-merge exercise. At specific locations in this document you will ultimately place special instructions known as *merge field names*, representing variable information that Word will insert into each copy of the document during the print merge.

♦ A *data file* containing the information for each personalized letter. In this exercise you'll create a data file called ORDERS.DOC to record special book orders placed by customers at Lantern Books. The most convenient way to organize these records is in table form. For the print merge process, each row of the table contains the information for one printed copy of the document—that is, the *record* of one customer's book order.

Once these two files are ready, you'll proceed through the three steps of the print merge:

1. Attach the data file, ORDERS.DOC, to the main document.

2. Insert the merge field names into the main document.

3. Instruct Word to begin merging the two files. Word prints one copy of the form letter for each record in ORDERS.DOC, replacing the merge field names in the main document with items of information from the data file.

CREATING A MAIN DOCUMENT

Figure 8.1 shows the main document for this print merge exercise. In this first version of the main document, you'll use the letters *XX* as temporary markers for the positions of the merge field names that you'll insert later. Follow these steps to create the document:

1. Open the BOOKLETR.DOC file from disk.

2. Replace the return address and the customer's name with rows of *XX* markers, as shown in Figure 8.1.

3. In the first paragraph, replace the book title and the price with *XX* markers. (Apply the bold italics style to the first marker in this paragraph.)

4. In the second paragraph, replace *election-related* with an *XX* marker. Delete the phrase *New titles include:* and the entire bulleted list below it.

5. Save the revised letter to disk as FORMLETR.DOC.

FIGURE 8.1:

The main document, with *XX* markers for variable information

Lantern Books
9898 Santa Barbara Avenue
San Francisco, CA 94000

2 June 1992

XX XX XX
XX

Dear XX XX:

We are happy to let you know that the book you ordered, *XX*, has arrived from the publisher. The price of the book is XX. Stop by to pick it up as soon as you can; we will hold it for three weeks.

While you are in, you may want to browse around and see some of the other XX titles we have recently received. Present this letter for a 10% discount on any additional book you decide to buy in this category.

Yours sincerely,

Bill and Mary Lantern
Lantern Books

There is nothing special about using the letters XX as temporary markers in this letter. You can use any characters you choose to mark the positions of the variable information in a print-merge document. As you'll see shortly, the purpose of these markers is to simplify the process of inserting merge field names into the letter.

CREATING A DATA FILE

In Figure 8.2 you see the data file for this exercise. Notice how the data table is organized. The first row of the table displays one word names that identify the data in each column: the customer's title (Dr., Ms., Mrs., Mr.), first name, last name, and address, the name of the book, the subject category, and the price. These names will eventually become the merge field names in your main document. Each subsequent row in the table contains the record of one book order. (To abbreviate the amount of typing you have to do, this file has only four order records; but the print-merge process works just the same regardless of the number of records in the data file.)

FIGURE 8.2:

The data file

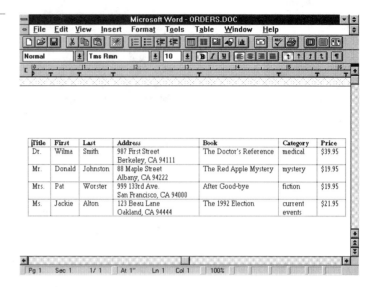

Title	First	Last	Address	Book	Category	Price
Dr.	Wilma	Smith	987 First Street Berkeley, CA 94111	The Doctor's Reference	medical	$39.95
Mr.	Donald	Johnston	88 Maple Street Albany, CA 94222	The Red Apple Mystery	mystery	$19.95
Mrs.	Pat	Worster	999 133rd Ave. San Francisco, CA 94000	After Good-bye	fiction	$19.95
Ms.	Jackie	Alton	123 Beau Lane Oakland, CA 94444	The 1992 Election	current events	$21.95

The terminology for the elements of the data file will be familiar to you if you have ever worked with a database management program: The columns in the data table are known as fields, and the one-word identifiers in the first row are the field names. The row of field names is sometimes called the header record, and subsequent rows are the data records.

Here are the steps for creating this data file:

1. Click the New button on the Toolbar to open a new document.

2. Using the Table button, insert a 5×7 table into the document—that is, a table with five rows and seven columns. Adjust the column widths in the table by dragging the **T** column markers in the ruler to the positions shown in Figure 8.2.

3. Enter the seven field names into the first row. Select the first row of the table and click the Bold button in the ribbon.

4. Enter the four order records into the next four rows of the table. Try not to type any extraneous spaces after the fields of information. In the fourth column, enter each address as a two-line field: Type the street address, press ↵, and then type the city, state, and zip code on the second line. As you enter the Address field for each record, Word automatically increases the height of the current row in the table. Do not press ↵ within any of the other fields.

5. Without entering any other text into the document, save the file to disk as ORDERS.DOC. Then choose File ➤ Close. (The data file does not need to be open during the print-merge process.)

You can use Tools ➤ Sorting to rearrange the records of a data table in any convenient order. For example, you might want to arrange the records of the ORDERS.DOC file in alphabetical order by the customers' names. To do so, you open the file and select the rows of data records in the table. (Do not include the header record in the selection.) Then choose Tools ➤ Sorting. In the Sorting dialog box, enter a value of 3—representing the third field, Last—into the Field Number box, and click OK. For more information see the reference entry **Sorting**.

SETTING UP THE PRINT MERGE DOCUMENT

Now you are ready to prepare your main document for the print-merge procedure. With FORMLETR.DOC displayed as the current document, follow these steps:

1. Choose File ➤ Print Merge. A pictorial dialog box called Print Merge Setup appears on the screen, as shown in Figure 8.3.

2. Click the Attach Data File button. In response, Word displays the Attach Data File dialog box, which is very similar to the Open dialog box.

3. In the File Name list, select the name of your data file, ORDERS.DOC, then click the OK button. Word does not open the data file, but attaches it to the main document file. In addition, Word displays a new option bar for FORMLETR.DOC, just above the ruler. The *print-merge bar*, shown in

FIGURE 8.3:

The Print Merge
Setup dialog box

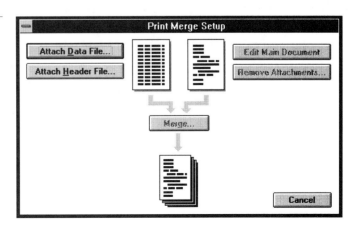

Figure 8.4, contains buttons for preparing and performing a print-merge operation. At the right side of the bar you can see the name of the attached data file, ORDERS.DOC.

4. Press Ctrl-Home, if necessary, to move the insertion point to the top of the document. Then choose Edit ➤ Find. Enter **XX** in the Find What text box, then click the Find Next button. Click Cancel to close the Find dialog box. In response to this command, Word highlights the first *XX* marker that you have placed in the main document.

5. Click the Insert Merge Field button on the print-merge bar. In the Insert Merge Field dialog box you see a list box named Print Merge Fields, as shown in Figure 8.5. This list contains the seven field names from the ORDERS.DOC data file. The first field, Title, is already highlighted in the list. Click OK to insert this selection into FORMLETR.DOC as the first merge field name. Back in the main document, Word displays this name inside double angle brackets (see Figure 8.6).

6. Press Shift-F4, the keyboard command for a Repeat Find operation. Word highlights the next *XX* marker in the document.

7. Repeat steps 5 and 6 eight times to insert the remaining merge field names into the document. In the Insert Merge Field dialog box, select the field names in this order: First, Last, Address, Title, Last, Book, Price, and Category. When you complete this part of the process, your main document appears as in Figure 8.6. As you can see, the document contains nine merge field names.

8. Click the Save button. FORMLETR.DOC is now a print-merge document, attached to the data file ORDERS.DOC.

The Attach Data File dialog box has a Create Data File button that you can click instead of choosing an existing data file from the File Name list. In response, Word walks you through the process of creating a data file, and provides some tools designed to simplify the task. The end result is the same as the data file you created at the beginning of this lesson—a file containing a data table for the print-merge process.

FIGURE 8.4:

The print merge bar

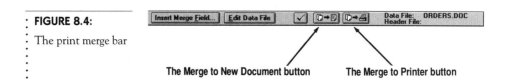

The Merge to New Document button   The Merge to Printer button

FIGURE 8.5:

The Insert Merge
Field dialog box

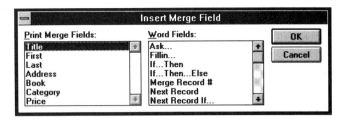

FIGURE 8.6:

The main
document with
merge field names

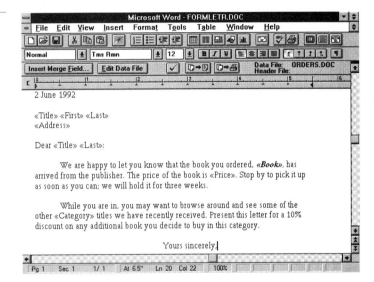

PERFORMING THE PRINT MERGE

The last button on the print-merge bar depicts a series of documents on their way to the printer; this is the Merge to Printer button. Now that you have completed preparations for the print merge, this is the button you press to begin the process:

1. Click the Merge to Printer button. The Print dialog box appears on the screen so you can select options for the upcoming print operation.

2. Click OK to start the process. Word prints one copy of your print-merge document for each record in the attached data file. In each printed copy, Word substitutes the merge field names with information from the data file.

For example, Figure 8.7 shows one personalized letter produced from the print-merge document you have created in this lesson. At the original positions of the nine merge field names, you can see information from the first order record in the ORDERS.DOC data file.

FIGURE 8.7:

A merged document

Lantern Books
9898 Santa Barbara Avenue
San Francisco, CA 94000

2 June 1992

Dr. Wilma Smith
987 First Street
Berkeley, CA 94111

Dear Dr. Smith:

We are happy to let you know that the book you ordered, ***The Doctor's Reference***, has arrived from the publisher. The price of the book is $39.95. Stop by to pick it up as soon as you can; we will hold it for three weeks.

While you are in, you may want to browse around and see some of the other medical titles we have recently received. Present this letter for a 10% discount on any additional book you decide to buy in this category.

Yours sincerely,

Bill and Mary Lantern
Lantern Books

TIP

Another option in the print-merge bar is the Merge to New Document button, located just to the left of the Merge to Printer button. If you click Merge to New Document, Word saves the merged documents in a document file instead of sending them to the printer. You might want to take advantage of this option if you want to make additional changes in the letters before you print them.

SUMMARY

In some businesses, the print-merge operation is the most important of all word processing functions. To prepare for a print merge, you attach a data file to a main document and you insert merge field names at appropriate positions in the text. The Print Merge Setup dialog box and the print-merge bar contain a variety of tools designed to simplify the process.

REFERENCE ENTRIES

See the following entries for more information:

Print Merge

Tables

Sorting

DEVELOPING SHORTCUTS

With features known as *templates*, *glossaries*, *macros*, and *styles*, Word gives you important ways to streamline your work. Using these features, you can devise your own special-purpose word-processing tools. A template serves as a pattern for a particular category of documents that you regularly create—for example, business letters, memos, reports, and so on. In a template file, you can store text, graphics, glossary entries, macros, and styles.

A glossary entry is a block of text or a graphic—or a combination of the two—that you use frequently in documents. By adding this entry to Word's glossary and giving the entry a name, you reduce the number of keystrokes necessary to insert the text or graphic into a document. A macro is a keyboard shortcut for performing a command or completing an action in Word. A style is a named collection of formatting instructions that you can add to the Style box in the ribbon.

In this final lesson you'll learn how these tools work, and see examples of each. You'll also take a brief look at Word's outlining capabilities, which give you a quick way to plan and organize a document.

CREATING AND USING A TEMPLATE

Every document you create in Word is based on a template. Word saves template files in the WINWORD directory, with the extension DOT. Up to now you've worked exclusively with Word's default template, NORMAL.DOT, which specifies the starting font, point size, margins, alignment, and indentation in a standard Word document. When you click the New button on the Toolbar, the resulting document is always based on this default template. By contrast, the File ➤ New command displays a list of all the templates available for creating a new document.

Word supplies a collection of templates designed for standard types of business letters and other documents. In addition, Word allows you to create your own templates and store them on disk for future use. For example, in the following exercise you'll create a letter template for Lantern Books. The template will include the bookstore's logo, name, and address, along with a special instruction that supplies the current date. In addition, the template will apply the margins and point sizes you have previously established in the document file BOOKLETR.DOC:

1. Open the BOOKLETR.DOC file. Delete the body of the letter—from the date to the line just above *Sincerely yours.*

2. Insert a blank line beneath the bookstore's return address. Choose Insert ➤ Date and Time and select the third option in the Available Formats box, as shown in Figure 9.1. This command enters a date *field* into the file; each time you open a new document based on this template, Word *updates* the field, producing a display of the current date.

FIGURE 9.1:

The Date and
Time dialog box

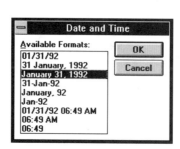

3. Choose File ➤ Save As. Pull down the Save File as Type list at the bottom of the Save As dialog box, and select the *Document Template (*.dot)* option. In response, Word automatically navigates to the WINWORD directory in the Directories box. Enter the name **LETTER** in the File Name text box and click OK.

4. The Summary Info dialog box appears next. Type **Letter template with bookstore logo** in the Title box and click OK. Word saves your new template as LETTER.DOT. Choose File ➤ Close to close the file.

A field is an instruction that tells Word to copy a particular item of information into a document. For example, the DATE and TIME fields read chronological information from the system calendar and clock. Another example is the PAGE field, which you inserted in the footer at the bottom of the newsletter you created in **Lesson 6***. When there is a change in the information that a field represents, you can update the result by moving the insertion point to the field and pressing F9. To see the full list of fields available in Word, choose Insert ➤ Field. For an explanation of a particular field, highlight the field in the Insert Field Type list and press F1. See* **Fields** *in* **Part II** *for more information.*

To create a new document based on the LETTER.DOT template, you select the template's name from the New dialog box:

1. Choose File ➤ New. The New dialog box appears.

2. Highlight the LETTER template in the Use Template list. As shown in Figure 9.2, the Description box displays the title you have entered into the template file's Summary Info box.

3. Click OK. Word opens a new document that contains the text and formatting from the LETTER.DOT template.

FIGURE 9.2:

The New dialog box

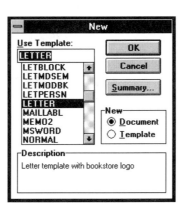

This new document is now ready to become a business letter under the bookstore's letterhead.

CREATING A GLOSSARY ENTRY

The glossary is one of the simplest yet most useful of all Word's time-saving devices. You create a glossary entry—and assign it a name—via Edit ➤ Glossary. The assigned name becomes the key to inserting the entry into a document.

TIP

You can create glossary entries either for global use or for exclusive use in documents based on a particular template. If the current document is based on a template other than NORMAL.DOT, Word prompts you to specify how you want to save a newly defined glossary entry. (This distinction also applies to macros.)

In the upcoming exercise you'll create a glossary entry to represent the logo and business name of Lantern Books.

1. In the current document, click in the selection bar just to the left of the bookstore's logo. This selects the line containing the logo along with the bookstore's name.

2. Choose Edit ➤ Glossary.

3. In the Glossary dialog box, enter the name **logo** into the Glossary Name text box, as in Figure 9.3. (Notice the description of the current selection at the bottom of the text box.)

4. Click the Define button.

5. A second dialog box appears over the first, as you see in Figure 9.4. Because the current document is based on the LETTER.DOT template, this dialog box gives you two options for determining the scope of your glossary

FIGURE 9.3:
The Glossary dialog box

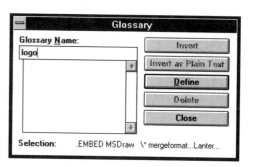

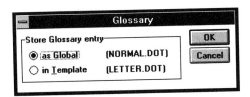

FIGURE 9.4:

Specifying the
location for a
glossary entry

entry: *as Global* (NORMAL.DOT) *or in Template* (LETTER.DOT). Click
OK to accept the default Global option.

Inserting a glossary entry into a document is easy: You simply type the entry's name
and press F3. Try it in the following steps:

1. Click the New button on the Toolbar to create a new document based on
    NORMAL.DOT.

2. Type **logo** at the top of the document.

3. Press F3. The bookstore logo and name appear in your document.

*If you can't remember the name you've assigned to a particular glossary entry, you can
use the Glossary command to insert the entry into a document: Choose Edit ➤ Glossary,
select the name you want from the Glossary Name list, and click the Insert button.*

CREATING AND USING MACROS

In its simplest form, a macro is a recording of the steps necessary to accomplish a
particular task in Word. To create such a recording you choose Tools ➤ Record
Macro and then you actually peform the steps. Word keeps track of your actions
until you stop the process by choosing the Stop Recorder command.

When you first create a macro, you assign it a name and a keyboard shortcut
key. (You also specify whether the macro should be stored globally or locally in a
particular template.) To perform a macro, you simply press the keyboard combination you have assigned it.

In the following exercise, you'll create two macros: one hides the Toolbar,
Ribbon, and Ruler all at once; the other brings these option bars back into view.
(The Toolbar, Ribbon, and Ruler entries in the View menu are the commands that
control the display of these three option bars.) As you go through the steps of this
exercise, you'll take a look at the features of Word's macro recorder:

1. Choose Tools ➤ Record Macro.

2. In the Record Macro dialog box, type the name **HideBars** (with no
    spaces) as the Record Macro Name entry. Then enter the letter **B** as the

Shortcut Key. (This means you'll be able to press Ctrl-Shift-B to perform the macro. A message in the Shortcut Key frame lets you know that this keyboard combination has not been assigned to any other macro.)

3. Enter the text **Hide the three option bars.** in the Description box. The Record Macro dialog box now appears as you see it in Figure 9.5. Click OK to begin the recording process. Word displays REC in the second-to-last panel of the status bar.

4. Pull down the View menu three times, and choose Toolbar, Ribbon, and Ruler in succession.

5. Choose Tools ➤ Stop Recorder.

6. Repeat steps 1 through 5, but this time enter **DisplayBars** (with no spaces) as the name of the second macro, **D** as the shortcut key, and **Display the three option bars.** as the description.

Now you can use these two macros whenever you want to hide or redisplay the three option bars: Press Ctrl-Shift-B to hide them (thus increasing the size of the text area), or Ctrl-Shift-D to bring them back again.

Tools ➤ Macro displays a list of all the global or template-specific macros currently available for your use. For example, the list box in Figure 9.6 shows the names of the two global macros you have just created. To run a macro, select its name in the list and click Run. To delete the selected macro, click the Delete button. To view the actual format in which Word has recorded a selected macro, click the Edit button.

DEFINING AND USING STYLES

A style is a useful combination of formats that you frequently apply to text in a document. The easiest way to create a style is by example: Apply the style first to a selection of text in the current document, then choose Format ➤ Style to assign a name to the style. After you have completed these steps, the new style name appears as an entry in the ribbon's drop-down Style list.

FIGURE 9.5:

The Record Macro dialog box

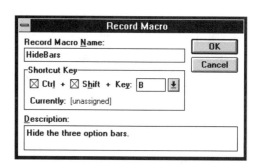

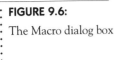

FIGURE 9.6:

The Macro dialog box

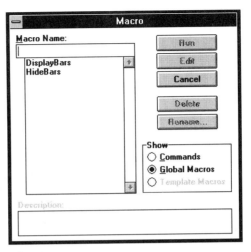

In the following exercise you'll create a style named Bordered, representing bold, centered, boxed text:

1. On a blank line in the current document, type your own name and press ↵.

2. Click in the selection bar to select the line containing your name.

3. Click the Bold button and then the Center button. Then choose Format ➤ Border and select the light double-line border. Click OK to apply this border to the current selection.

4. Without changing the selection in your document, choose Format ➤ Style. When the Style dialog box appears, enter **Bordered** in the Style Name box. Then click the Define button to expand the dialog box. As you see in Figure 9.7, the *Description (by example)* box shows the combination of styles applied to the current text selection.

5. Click the *Add to Template* option, placing an X in the corresponding check box.

6. After clicking the Add to check box, click the Add button. Then click the Close button to close the dialog box.

Now if you pull down the Style list in the ribbon, you'll find the new Bordered style as one of the entries in the list. You can now apply this style to any line or block of text in a document. For example, try this experiment:

1. Enter the name of your city on a blank line in the current document.

2. Pull down the Style list and choose the Bordered style. In response, Word applies the combination of styles to the new text: boldfaced, centered, and bordered.

FIGURE 9.7:

The Style dialog box

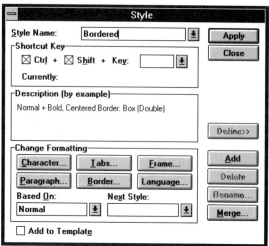

3. Close both of the documents you have been working on in this lesson. You do not need to save them.

USING STYLES IN OUTLINING

Outlining is one important application for Word's default list of styles. Outlining is an efficient way to plan the structure of headings and subheadings in a document before you begin writing the text. As you create an outline, Word applies default styles from the Styles list to the various levels of headings you write.

To begin an outline, you choose View ➤ Outline. In response, Word displays an Outline bar above the text area, as shown in Figure 9.8. You use the first two buttons in this bar to promote or demote headings; as you do so, Word applies default styles (named *heading 1*, *heading 2*, *heading 3*, and so on) to specific heading levels.

For example, Figure 9.9 shows the beginning of an outline, with four levels of headings. After you've begun an outline like this one, the buttons in the Outline bar make it easy to change the levels and the positions of the headings. When you are ready to type an actual block of text under a heading, you click the fifth button to demote a heading to the level of *body text*. The ten buttons on the right side of the Outline bar allow you to restrict the view of your outline to a specific level of headings. Finally, when you are ready to view and print your document in non-outline form, you simply switch to Normal or Page Layout view.

For more information about outlining, see the **Outlining** *entry in* **Part II**.

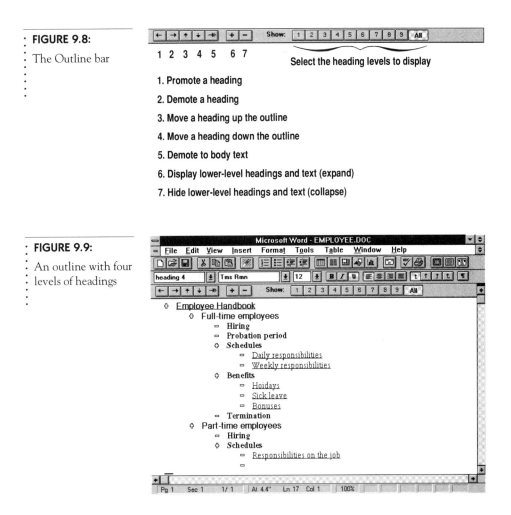

FIGURE 9.8:

The Outline bar

1 2 3 4 5   6 7

Select the heading levels to display

1. Promote a heading

2. Demote a heading

3. Move a heading up the outline

4. Move a heading down the outline

5. Demote to body text

6. Display lower-level headings and text (expand)

7. Hide lower-level headings and text (collapse)

FIGURE 9.9:

An outline with four levels of headings

CONFIRMING THE MACRO AND GLOSSARY CHANGES

At the end of a session in which you have created new global macros or glossary entries, Word asks you to confirm that you want to save these changes to disk for use in subsequent sessions. When you choose File ➤ Exit, Word displays the dialog box shown in Figure 9.10. To save your changes, click the Yes button. In response, Word makes appropriate changes in the NORMAL.DOT file before exiting.

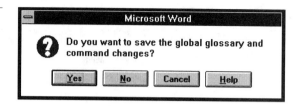

FIGURE 9.10:
Confirming
global changes

SUMMARY

The more you learn about Word's special time-saving devices—such as custom templates, glossary entries, macros, styles, and outlining—the more efficiently you can create documents. All of these tools are optional: You use them only when they seem appropriate in the context of your own work. Creatively applied, they allow you to fashion a word processing environment that responds to your needs and requirements.

REFERENCE ENTRIES

See the following entries for more information about shortcut techniques in Word:

- *Fields*
- *Glossary Entries*
- *Macros*
- *Outlining*
- *Styles*
- *Templates*

PART TWO

REFERENCE

ALIGNING

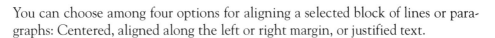

You can choose among four options for aligning a selected block of lines or paragraphs: Centered, aligned along the left or right margin, or justified text.

TO ALIGN A SELECTED BLOCK OF TEXT

1. Select the text and choose Format ➤ Paragraph.
2. Pull down the Alignment list and choose one of the four options: Left, Centered, Right, or Justified.
3. Click OK.

Shortcuts: Select the text and then click one of the four alignment buttons in the ribbon, or press Ctrl-L (for left-aligned text), Ctrl-E (for centered text), Ctrl-R (for right-aligned text), or Ctrl-J (for justified text).

EXAMPLES

Here are examples of the four text alignment options:

In **left-aligned** text, each line is flush against the left border, but the lines break at uneven points along the right border.

In **centered** text, each line of a paragraph is centered between the left and right margins. The length of each line is determined by word breaks.

In **right-aligned** text, each line is flush against the right border. The left side of the block of text is uneven. This is sometimes called *ragged left*.

In **justified** text, the lines of a paragraph are aligned along both the left and right margins. Word automatically inserts extra space between words in order to accomplish this effect.

NOTE

If you choose an alignment option before you begin typing a paragraph, word-wrap occurs within the alignment you have chosen.

SEE ALSO

Formatting Paragraphs, Selecting Text

ALPHABETIC CASE

Word provides keyboard shortcuts for changing the letters in a selection of text to specific combinations of uppercase and lowercase.

TO CHANGE THE ALPHABETIC CASE IN A SELECTION OF TEXT

Select the text and press Shift-F3 one or more times until you see the case pattern you want.

EXAMPLES

The selection *Desktop Publishing* changes to the following case combinations each time you press Shift-F3:

desktop publishing

DESKTOP PUBLISHING

Desktop Publishing

NOTE

Press Ctrl-A to change a selection of text to all uppercase.

SEE ALSO

Selecting Text

ANNOTATIONS

Annotations provide a simple way for reviewers and editors to communicate with an author, by inserting remarks, suggestions, explanations, criticisms, clarifications, or opinions into a document. Annotations become part of the document, but Word keeps them separate from the main text and displays them in a special *annotation pane*. You can insert new annotations, view existing ones, copy the text of an annotation into your document, or delete an annotation from a file.

TO INSERT AN ANNOTATION AT THE CURRENT POSITION IN A DOCUMENT

1. Choose Insert ➤ Annotation. Word opens the annotation pane and inserts an *annotation mark* both at the insertion point in the document and at the next position in the annotation pane. (An annotation mark consists of your initials along with the number of the current annotation, both enclosed in square brackets.)

2. Type a note or comment of any length, starting from the insertion mark in the annotation pane.

3. Click the Close button at the top of the annotation pane. In response, Word closes the annotation pane and hides the annotation mark in the document.

EXAMPLE

The default initials for annotation marks come from the name that you entered when you installed Word on your computer. For the registered name *Mary Lantern*, Word produces the annotation marks *[ML1]*, *[ML2]*, *[ML3]*, and so on.

NOTE

To change the default initials for annotation marks, choose Tools ➤ Options, click the User Info icon in the Category list, and revise the entry in the Initials text box.

TO VIEW THE ANNOTATIONS IN A DOCUMENT

Choose View ➤ Annotations. Word opens the annotations pane, where you can scroll down the sequence of annotations.

Shortcut: Click the Show/Hide ¶ button on the ribbon; the annotation marks appear along with other special characters that are normally hidden. Double-click any annotation mark. Word opens the annotation pane and scrolls directly to the annotation you have selected.

NOTE

If the Annotations command is dimmed in the View menu, the active document contains no annotations.

TO COPY AN ANNOTATION INTO THE DOCUMENT

1. Choose View ➤ Annotations and scroll down to the annotation you want to copy.

2. Select the text of the annotation, *without* the annotation mark.

3. Use the Copy and Paste buttons to copy the text from the annotation pane to a selected position in the document pane.

NOTE

To move between panes, press F6 or click the mouse in the pane that you want to activate.

TO DELETE AN ANNOTATION

1. Click the Show/Hide ¶ button to view the annotation marks and double-click the mark for the annotation you are planning to delete. In the annotation pane, examine the text of the annotation to confirm that you want to delete it.

2. Select the annotation mark in the *document* pane and press Del.

SEE ALSO

Copying Text, Go To, Hiding Text, Options for Word Settings, Panes, Special Characters

BACKUPS

Word can create a backup file containing the previous version of your document each time you perform a Save operation. You activate the backup option from the Options dialog box.

TO ACTIVATE THE BACKUP OPTION

1. Choose Tools ➤ Options.
2. Click the Save icon in the Category list.
3. Click the Always Create Backup Copy option, placing an X in the corresponding check box. Then click OK.

EXAMPLE

Suppose you are saving a file named MEMO.DOC. If the backup option is on, Word saves the backup of this file as MEMO.BAK.

NOTE

The backup option is off by default when you first install Word for Windows.

SEE ALSO

Deleting a Document from Disk, Finding a File, Opening a File, Saving, Options for Word Settings

BOOKMARKS

A bookmark is a name that you define for a particular location or selection of text in a document. Once you have defined a bookmark, you can use Word's Go To command to jump quickly to the named location or to select the named block of text. (Bookmarks are also essential in several other Word procedures, such as inserting a block of text from one document into another, creating a link between two document files, performing calculations, and inserting cross-reference fields into a document.)

TO DEFINE A BOOKMARK

1. Move the insertion point to the location you want to mark or select the block of text that you want to identify.

2. Choose Insert ➤ Bookmark.

3. In the Bookmark Name text box, enter the name for the bookmark. Then click OK.

Shortcut: Position the insertion point or select the target text, then press Ctrl-Shift-F5. In response, Word displays the prompt *Insert bookmark:* at the beginning of the status bar. Enter a name for the new bookmark and press ↵.

EXAMPLE

Imagine that you are working on a long document containing three important data tables. As you write, you need to look back frequently at the tables and study the information they contain. To simplify the process of finding the tables, you insert a bookmark at the beginning of each table, assigning them the names *T1*, *T2*, and *T3*. Once you've defined these bookmarks, you can use the Go To command to jump to any one of the tables when you need to review it.

NOTE

A bookmark name must begin with a letter of the alphabet and can contain letters, digits, and underscore characters. The maximum length is 20 characters. Alphabetic case is not significant.

TO GO TO THE LOCATION
OR SELECTION REPRESENTED BY A BOOKMARK

1. Choose Edit ➤ Go To. The Go To dialog box displays a list of all the bookmarks defined for the current document.

2. Select a bookmark from the list of names and click OK. (Or, simply double-click a name in the list.) If the bookmark represents a location, Word moves the insertion point to the location. If the bookmark represents a block of text, Word moves to the text and selects it.

Shortcuts: The F5 function key is a shortcut for the Go To command. When you press F5, Word displays the prompt *Go To:* in the status bar. To go to the location of a defined bookmark, enter the name directly into the status bar and press ↵.

(To display the Go To dialog box on the screen, press F5 twice or double-click the mouse anywhere inside the status bar.)

EXAMPLE

To move quickly to the location of a bookmark named T1, press F5 and enter **T1** into the status bar. Then press ↵.

SEE ALSO

Calculations, Fields, Go To, Inserting a File, Links

BORDERS

Using the Border command, you can display single-line or double-line borders around any text or graphic selection. In addition, you can add the visual illusion of shadowing behind the border and apply colored shading within the perimeter of the border. You can also use the Border command to display vertical or horizontal lines along one or more sides of a selection.

TO DISPLAY A BORDER AROUND A SELECTION

1. Select the text or graphics where you want to place the border. (If you want the border to appear around only one paragraph, you can simply move the insertion point into the paragraph.)

2. Choose Format ➤ Border. The Border dialog box has three groups of options in frames, labeled Border, Preset, and Line.

3. Click one of the available border styles displayed in the Line box. Optionally, pull down the Color list and choose a color or shade of gray for the border itself. The Border box displays a model of the border style you have chosen.

4. If you want to adjust the amount of space between the border and the text inside the border, change the numeric From Text setting in the Border box. (The default is 1 point.)

5. If you want a shadow to appear behind the border, click the Shadow option in the Preset box.

6. Click OK.

EXAMPLES

Here are examples of a selection of border styles, with and without shadows:

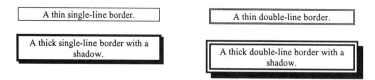

NOTE

To change the horizontal width of a border displayed around a selection, you can adjust the margin markers on the ruler.

TO DISPLAY A LINE ALONG ONE OR MORE SIDES OF A SELECTION

1. Select the text and/or graphics where you want the line to appear and choose Format ➤Border.

2. In the Preset box, click the None option if it is not already selected.

3. In the model displayed in the Border box, click the side where you want the border to appear—top, bottom, left, right, or between paragraphs. To display a line along more than one side, hold down the Shift key and click the additional side or sides.

4. Click a border style in the Line box; then click OK.

EXAMPLES

Here are some line examples, all created with the Border command:

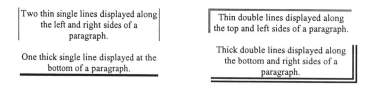

SEE ALSO

Colors, Frames, Margins, Shading, Tables

BULLETED LISTS

In a bulleted list, Word displays a bullet symbol at the beginning of each line or paragraph. By default, paragraphs in a bulleted list are formatted with *hanging indents*.

TO CREATE A BULLETED LIST

1. Select the sequence of lines or paragraphs that you want to include in the list, and then Choose Tools ➤ Bullets and Numbering.

2. At the top of the Bullets and Numbering dialog box, click the Bullets option button if it is not already selected.

3. In the Bullet Character box, choose the bullet symbol that you want to use in the list. Optionally, adjust the numeric setting in the Point Size box to change the display size of the selected bullet.

4. If you want a larger or smaller indent for paragraphs in the list, adjust the setting in the Hanging Indent By text box. (If you do not want the paragraphs in the list to be formatted as hanging indents, click the Hanging Indent By option to remove the X from the check box.) The Sample box shows a model of the bulleted list you are creating.

5. Click OK.

Shortcut: Select the lines or paragraphs of the list and click the Bulleted List button in the Toolbar. Word applies the bullet symbol and the hanging indent format currently selected in the Bulleted List dialog box.

EXAMPLES

Here are examples of bulleted lists formatted with and without hanging indents.

- The paragraphs in this bulleted list are formatted as hanging indents.
- The first line of each paragraph appears further to the left than the remaining lines.
- As a result, the bullet symbols are aligned at the left of the paragraphs.

➡ The paragraphs in this list are not formatted as hanging indents.
➡ As a result, the bullet symbols are aligned with the left margin of the text.
➡ Notice the non-default bullet symbol in this list.
➡ This symbol was selected from the Symbol dialog box.

NOTES

To select a new bullet symbol for bulleted lists, choose Tools ➤ Bullets and Numbering, click the Bullets option, and then click the New Bullet button in the Bullet

Character box. The resulting Symbol dialog box displays a large selection of special symbols, some of which are appropriate for use in bulleted lists.

When you create a bulleted list, Word inserts a SYMBOL field at the beginning of each paragraph in the list. Choose View ➤ Field Codes to see the field codes that produce the bullet characters.

SEE ALSO

Fields, Hanging Indents, Indenting, Numbered Lists, Symbols

CALCULATIONS

Using the Calculate command, you can find the sum of a sequence of numbers in your document or the result of an arithmetic expression. In addition, you can use bookmarks and the EXPRESSION field to perform arithmetic operations on numbers located in different places within your document.

TO FIND THE SUM OF A SEQUENCE OF NUMBERS

1. Select the text that contains the numbers. If the numbers are arranged in a tabbed column, hold down the *right* mouse button and select the column by dragging the mouse. (Word ignores any non-numeric text that appears in the selection.)

2. Choose Tools ➤ Calculate. Word briefly displays the sum of the numbers in the status bar and copies the sum to the Clipboard.

3. To insert the sum into your document, move the insertion point to the target location and click the Paste button in the Toolbar.

EXAMPLE

The following list shows how you can use the Calculate command to find the sum of numbers arranged in a tabbed column:

Californians and the National Election	$7.45
The 1992 Election Year	$19.95
How Women Vote	$9.95
Total	**$37.35**

To compute the total, select the numbers in the first three lines and choose Tools ➤ Calculate; then move the insertion point to the end of the **Total** line and click the Paste button.

NOTE

If any number in the selection contains a dollar sign, the Calculate command includes a dollar sign in the result.

TO FIND THE RESULT OF
AN ARITHMETIC EXPRESSION

1. Type a sequence of numbers and arithmetic operators into your document.

2. Select the numbers and operators and choose Tools ➤ Calculate.

3. Move the insertion point to the location where you want to insert the result and click the Paste button.

EXAMPLE

The following example shows how you can use the Calculate command to find the result of an expression:

(19.75 + 22.87 - 8.19) * .95 = **32.71**

To calculate the result, select the expression at the left of the equal sign and choose Tools ➤ Calculate. Then move the insertion point to the position after the equal sign and click the Paste button.

TO PERFORM A CALCULATION ON NUMBERS
FROM DIFFERENT LOCATIONS IN A DOCUMENT

1. Assign a bookmark name to each number that you want to include in the calculation. (Select each number in turn and choose Insert ➤ Bookmark.)

2. Move the insertion point to the location where you want to enter the result of the calculation.

3. Choose Insert ➤ Field and select the = *expression* field in the Insert Field Type list.

4. Enter the arithmetic expression—using the bookmark names to represent numeric values in your document—into the Field Code text box.

5. Click OK. If your document displays the field codes rather than the result, choose View ➤ Field Codes.

EXAMPLE

The following EXPRESSION field calculates 90% of the sum of four numbers from various locations in a document, where the numbers are assigned bookmark names of *price1*, *price2*, *price3*, and *price4*:

{= .9*(price1+price2+price3+price4)}

SEE ALSO

Bookmarks, Fields, Selecting Text, Tables

CLOSING A DOCUMENT

Regardless of the number of documents open at a given time in Word, you can close each document individually when you are finished with it. If you have made changes in the document, Word gives you the option of saving the changes to disk or closing without saving.

TO CLOSE THE CURRENT DOCUMENT WINDOW

1. Choose File ➤ Close.
2. If you have made changes in the document since the last save, Word displays a dialog box asking if you want to save the changes. Click Yes to save or No to abandon the changes.

Shortcut: To close any document, double-click the control-menu box at the upper-left corner of the document window.

NOTES

To close a document that is not in the active window, pull down the Window menu and choose the document's name in the menu list. This activates the file, bringing it to the foreground. Then choose the Close command.

If you close all open documents, Word's menu bar displays only the File and Help menus.

SEE ALSO

Saving, Opening a File, Window Arrangements

COLORS

With the appropriate hardware—a color monitor and a color printer—you can display and print the text of a document in a variety of colors.

TO CHANGE THE COLOR OF A TEXT SELECTION

1. Select the text and choose Format ➤ Character.
2. Pull down the Color list and choose a color.
3. Then click OK.

SEE ALSO

Printing, Shading

COLUMNS

Word allows you to format all or part of your document in newspaper-style columns. Column formatting applies to a particular *section* of your document; different sections can contain different numbers of columns. (If there are no section breaks, the column formatting applies to the entire document.)

TO ORGANIZE A SECTION OF TEXT INTO NEWSPAPER-STYLE COLUMNS

1. If necessary, choose Insert ➤ Break one or more times to insert section breaks at appropriate points in your document. (You must position the insertion point before creating each break.) Then move the insertion point into the target section and choose Format ➤ Columns.
2. Adjust the setting in the Number of Columns box. When you do so, the Sample box shows you how the resulting columns of text will appear in your document.
3. Optionally, adjust the setting in the Space Between box to increase or decrease the space between the columns. Click the Line Between option if you want a vertical line to appear between the columns.
4. Click OK to apply the column formatting. Choose View ➤ Page Layout to see how your columns will appear on the printed page, or choose File ➤ Print Preview to view the complete effect of columns and the lines displayed between them.

Shortcut: Move the insertion point into the target section of your document, and click the Text Columns button in the Toolbar. In the graphic that appears beneath the button, drag the mouse across the number of columns you want to apply to the

section. (As you do so, the caption beneath the graphic tells you the number of columns you have selected.) Release the mouse button to apply the column formatting.

EXAMPLE

In *Lesson 5*, Figures 5.1, 5.2, and 5.8 illustrate a document organized in columns.

NOTE

You can apply column formatting to a selection of text, without first inserting section breaks: Select the text, choose Format ➤ Columns, and adjust the Number of Columns setting. Then pull down the Apply To list and choose the Selected Text option. Click OK. Word automatically inserts section breaks at the beginning and the end of your text selection, and applies the column formatting to the section.

TO BREAK A COLUMN AT A SELECTED POINT IN THE TEXT

1. Move the insertion point to the position where you want a given column to end and choose Insert ➤ Break.

2. In the Break dialog box, click the Column Break option and then click OK.

TO DIVIDE THE TEXT EVENLY AMONG THE COLUMNS IN A SECTION

1. Move the insertion point to the end of the text in the last column.

2. Choose Insert ➤ Break. In the Break dialog box, choose the Continuous option in the Section Break frame.

SEE ALSO

Page Breaks, Page Layout View, Previewing, Sections, Selecting Text

CONVERTING DOCUMENT FORMATS

Word can save documents in file formats used by other major application programs. Conversely, Word can read files that you have created in other software environments and convert them into Word documents.

TO CONVERT A WORD DOCUMENT INTO ANOTHER FILE FORMAT

1. Open the Word document file that you want to convert.
2. Choose File ➤ Save As.
3. In the Save As dialog box, pull down the Save File as Type list and choose the file format in which you want to save the file.
4. In the File Name text box, type a new name for the file conversion. Then click OK.

TO READ AND CONVERT A FILE THAT WAS CREATED IN ANOTHER SOFTWARE ENVIRONMENT

1. Choose File ➤ Open.
2. Enter the name of the file in the File Name text box. (If necessary, use the Directories and Drives boxes to specify the correct path for the target file.) Click OK. Word displays the Convert File dialog box whenever you attempt to open a file that is not in normal Word format.
3. In the Convert File dialog box, select the format in which the file is currently stored and click OK.

SEE ALSO

Opening a File, Saving

COPYING STYLES

Word supplies a quick keyboard-and-mouse technique for copying text styles—such as bold, italics, underlining, font, and point size—from one text selection to another.

TO COPY CHARACTER FORMATS

1. Select the text where you want to apply the copied styles.
2. Hold down the Ctrl and Shift keys together.
3. Position the mouse pointer over a character that already has the formatting you want to apply to the selected text and click the *left* mouse button. (The *right* mouse button has a different use when you press Ctrl-Shift; see *Copying Text* for details.)

NOTE

This technique copies text formats that you select from the Format ➤ Character command.

SEE ALSO

Fonts, Formatting Text, Point Size, Ribbon, Styles

COPYING TEXT

You can use the Clipboard to copy text from one place to another within a document or from one document to another.

TO COPY TEXT

1. Select the text that you want to copy.
2. Click the Copy button in the Toolbar or choose Edit ➤ Copy. This action copies the selection to the Clipboard.

3. Move the insertion point to the position where you want to copy the text. (To copy the text to another open document, choose the document's name from the Window menu.)

4. Click the Paste button or choose Edit ➤ Paste.

Shortcut: Select the text you want to copy, then hold down Ctrl-Shift and click the right mouse button at the destination. This shortcut does not use the Clipboard.

NOTES

As long as a selection remains in the Clipboard, you can use the Paste command to make multiple copies at any number of destinations. You can also use the Clipboard to copy a selection from Word to another Windows application.

SEE ALSO

Deleting Text, Moving Text, Spike

DASHES

Word provides special codes for entering an en dash or em dash into a document. You type these codes on the numeric keypad.

TO ENTER A DASH

1. If necessary, press Num Lock to activate the numeric keypad. (*NUM* appears in the status bar.)
2. Hold down the Alt key and type a four-digit code at the numeric keypad:
   - Alt-0150 for an en dash.
   - Alt-0151 for an em dash.
3. Optionally, press Num Lock again to deactivate the keypad. (NUM disappears from the status bar.)

NOTE

If you use dashes frequently in your writing, you'll probably want to create a macro to enter the en dash or the em dash into a document.

SEE ALSO

Macros, Quotation Marks, Symbols

DATE AND TIME ENTRIES

The Date and Time command provides a selection of formats for entering the current date and time into a document. When you choose this command, Word inserts a TIME field, which reads the date and time from the system calendar and clock. You can update this field at any time.

TO ENTER A DATE OR TIME FIELD

1. Choose Insert ➤ Date and Time. The Date and Time dialog box appears.
2. Choose a date, time, or combination format from the Available Formats list, then click OK.

EXAMPLE

Here are examples of date, time, and combination formats produced by the Date and Time command:

- Date formats: 08/10/92; August 10, 1992; 10-Aug-92
- Time formats: 09:49 PM; 21:49
- Combination format: 08/10/92 09:49 PM

TO UPDATE A DATE OR TIME FIELD

Move the insertion point into the field and press F9.

SEE ALSO

Fields, Headers and Footers

DELETING A DOCUMENT FROM DISK

The Find File command allows you to delete document files from disk while Word is running.

TO DELETE A DOCUMENT FILE

1. Choose File ➤ Find File. In the File Find dialog box, the File Name box lists the files in the current search path and the Contents box shows the actual text in the currently selected document file.

2. If the file that you want to delete is not listed in the File Name box, click the Search button. In the resulting Search dialog box, enter a new search path in the Path text box, then click the Start Search button.

3. Back in the Find File dialog box, select the name of the file you want to delete. Examine the Contents box to confirm that you have chosen the right file.

4. Click the Delete button. Word next asks you to confirm the operation; click the Yes button to delete the file.

5. Click the Close button to close the Find File dialog box.

NOTE

To highlight multiple files in the File Find dialog box, hold down the Ctrl key while you click the files you want to include in the selection. When you click the Delete key, Word asks you to confirm that you want to delete the selected files. Click Yes to delete all the files at once.

SEE ALSO

Finding a File, Opening a File

DELETING TEXT

Word provides several keyboard and mouse techniques for deleting text from the current document.

TO DELETE TEXT

- ◆ Press Backspace to delete the character before the insertion point.
- ◆ Press Del to delete the character after the insertion point.
- ◆ Press Ctrl-Backspace to delete the word before the insertion point.
- ◆ Press Ctrl-Delete to delete the word after the insertion point.
- ◆ Select a block of text and press Del to delete the selection.
- ◆ Click the Cut button to delete a selection and copy it to the Clipboard.

NOTE

Click the Undo button or press Ctrl-Z to undo the last deletion.

SEE ALSO

Undoing an Operation

DRAFT MODE

Draft mode allows you to work efficiently with a complex document—for example a document that contains embedded graphic objects. In Draft mode, Word displays empty frames in the place of embedded objects and uses underlining to indicate all text formatting.

TO ACTIVATE DRAFT MODE

Choose View ➤ Draft. (If you were previously working in Page Layout view, Word switches you into Normal view.)

NOTE

The View ➤ Draft command is a toggle. Choose the same command again to de-activate Draft mode.

SEE ALSO

Normal View, Page Layout View, Printing

DRAW

In the Draw program you can create artwork and logos to incorporate into a Word document. The resulting graphic is inserted into your document as an *embedded object*.

TO CREATE A DRAWING IN MICROSOFT DRAW

1. Move the insertion point to where you want to insert the drawing.
2. Choose Insert ➤ Object. The Object dialog box appears.
3. In the Object Type list box, choose the Microsoft Drawing option and then click OK. After a few seconds, the Draw application window appears.
4. Use the drawing tools in Draw to create your artwork—the line tool, the ellipse/circle tool, the rounded rectangle tool, the rectangle tool, the arc tool, the freeform tool, and the text tool.

5. When you have completed your drawing, choose File ➤ Exit and Return from Draw's menu bar. A dialog box asks you whether you want to update your Word document; click Yes.

Shortcut: Click the Draw button in the Toolbar to start Microsoft Draw.

EXAMPLE

For an example of a logo created in Draw, see Figures 6.1, 6.5, and 6.6 in *Lesson 6*.

NOTE

Choose Help ➤ How To in the Draw menu bar for a list of general and introductory help topics.

TO CHANGE THE SIZE AND SHAPE OF A GRAPHIC

1. Click the object to select it. Word encloses the graphic in a border and displays eight sizing handles around the perimeter.
2. Drag any one of the sizing handles to increase or decrease the size.

TO EDIT A DRAWING

Double-click the drawing in the document window. This restarts Draw and copies the drawing back into the Draw application window.

SEE ALSO

Embedded Objects, Equation Editor, Frame, Graph, WordArt

EMBEDDED OBJECTS

Word comes with four programs that you can use to insert drawings, charts, equations, and special typographical effects into a document. The programs are called Draw, Graph, Equation Editor, and WordArt.

TO INSERT AN EMBEDDED OBJECT

Choose Insert ➤ Object. Then choose an option in the Object Type list and click OK. The corresponding application window appears on the screen. Create the object and then choose File ➤ Exit and Return from the application's menu bar. (In WordArt, click the OK button.) Click Yes in response to the Update prompt.

NOTE

When you create an object with one of these programs, Word inserts the result into your document as an EMBED field. If you see fields codes instead of the object, press Shift-F9.

SEE ALSO

Draw, Fields, Equation Editor, Graph, WordArt

EQUATION EDITOR

In the Equation Editor you can combine the symbols and operands of complex mathematical equations for display in technical documents.

TO CREATE AN EQUATION IN THE EQUATION EDITOR

1. Move the insertion point to where you want to insert the equation.
2. Choose Insert ➤ Object. In the Object Type list box, choose the Equation option and then click OK. After a few seconds, the Equation Editor application window appears.
3. Use the tools in the Equation Editor to create your equation.

4. When you have completed the equation, choose File ➤ Exit and Return from the Equation Editor's menu bar. A dialog box asks you whether you want to update your Word document; click Yes.

EXAMPLE

Here is an example of an equation created in the Equation Editor application window:

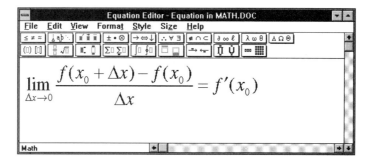

The two rows of buttons located between the menu bar and the work area supply you with selections of mathematical symbols, Greek letters, subscripting and super-scripting options, and other technical operands.

NOTE

Choose Help ➤ Procedures in the Equation Editor's menu bar for a list of general and introductory help topics.

TO EDIT AN EQUATION

Double-click the object in the document window. This restarts the Equation Editor and copies the equation back into the application window.

SEE ALSO

Draw, Embedded Objects, Graph, WordArt

EXITING

The Exit command closes the Word application window and ends your current session with Word.

TO EXIT WORD

Choose File ➤ Exit. (If any open documents contain unsaved changes, Word asks you whether you want to save the changes before exiting.)

Shortcuts: Double-click the control-menu box at the upper-left corner of the application window, or press Alt-F4.

NOTE

If you have created global macros or glossary entries in the current session, Word asks you whether you want to update these changes. If you click Yes, these global elements will be available to you in subsequent sessions with word.

SEE ALSO

Glossary Entries, Macros, Saving

FIELDS

A field is a special tool that obtains information from an identified source and displays it at a location in a document. The Field command gives you access to Word's many fields; to insert a field, you select its name from the Field dialog box. You can *update* the result of a field whenever you think there might be a change in the information's source. Field *codes* are enclosed in braces, { and }; they consist of a field's name along with instructions that tell Word where to get information or how to handle it. In a document that contains fields, you can view either the field codes or the *field results*—that is, the information that the field obtains.

(In the context of Word's Print Merge feature, the term *field* has a second meaning. In a data file, a field is a column of information and a *field name* is the identifier at the top of a column. See *Lesson 8* or the *Print Merge* entry for more information.)

TO INSERT A FIELD

1. Move the insertion point to where you want to enter the field and then choose Insert ➤ Field.

2. Scroll down the Insert Field Type list and select the name of the field you want to insert into your document. Word inserts the field name into the Field Code text box, and displays any relevant options in the Instructions list. (Press F1 to open a Help topic describing the field you have selected.)

3. Optionally, select an item from the Instructions list and click Add. Then enter relevant information into the Field Code text box.

4. Click OK. Depending on the current setting of the View ➤ Field Codes command, Word displays either the field codes or the result of the field at the current location in your document.

EXAMPLE

The following DATE field reads the current date from the system calendar and displays it in a long format:

    {date \@ "dddd, MMMM d, yyyy"}

To enter this field, choose Insert ➤ Field and select *date* from the Insert Field Type list. (You can press *D* twice from the keyboard to scroll quickly down to this field in the list.) Then select the format displayed as *MMMM d, yyyy* in the Instructions list and click the Add button. Finally, enter **dddd** just after the first quotation mark in the Field Code text box and click OK. The result of this field entry appears in the following format:

Tuesday, August 11, 1992

(The actual date depends upon the current setting of your system's calendar.)

NOTES

Several Word operations automatically insert fields. For example, when you click the Bulleted List button, Word inserts SYMBOL fields to obtain the appropriate symbols for the bullets themselves.

If you know the code format for a field, you can use this technique to enter the field into your document:

1. Move the insertion point to the location where you want to enter the field, and press Ctrl-F9. Word inserts an empty field, represented by a pair of braces, { }. The insertion point appears inside the braces.

2. Enter the name of the field, along with any relevant field instructions.

3. Press Shift-F9 to view the result of the field.

TO UPDATE A FIELD

Move the insertion point to the field and press F9.

TO TOGGLE BETWEEN THE DISPLAY OF FIELD CODES AND FIELD RESULTS

Choose View ➤ Field Codes.

Shortcut: Press Shift-F9.

TO PREVENT WORD FROM UPDATING A FIELD

Move the insertion point into the field and press Ctrl-F11. This is called *locking* a field. As long as a field is locked, it retains its current result.

TO UNLOCK A FIELD
SO THAT IT CAN BE UPDATED AGAIN

Move the insertion point into the field and press Ctrl-Shift-F11.

TO CONVERT A FIELD TO ITS RESULT

Move the insertion point into the field and press Ctrl-Shift-F9. This is called *unlinking* a field from its source. After you unlink a field, the result can no longer be updated.

SEE ALSO

Calculations, Date and Time Entries, Embedded Objects, Links, Print Merge, Symbols

FINDING A FILE

The Find File command is a powerful and versatile Word feature that helps you locate and preview document files stored on disk. You can also use this command to open, delete, copy, or print a selection of one or more files.

TO VIEW INFORMATION
ABOUT A SELECTION OF FILES

1. Choose File ➤ Find File. Find File initially displays a list of files from the path or paths identified at the upper-left corner of the dialog box.

2. Click the Search button to change the selection of files listed in the File Name box. In the resulting Search dialog box you can expand or restrict the file search as follows:

   ◆ Enter a file name pattern into the File Name box (or make a selection from the Type list) to restrict the search to files of a certain type.

   ◆ Enter a list of search paths—placing a semicolon between each path—into the Path box, to expand the search to additional directories. (Alternatively, click the Edit Path button to open a dialog box designed to help you create the list of search paths.)

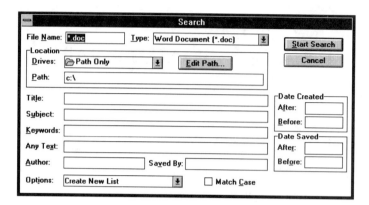

- ◆ Enter information into the Title, Subject, Keywords, Author, and Saved By text boxes to restrict the search to files with specific entries in their Summary Info boxes.

- ◆ Enter text into the Any Text box to restrict the search to documents that contain the text you specify.

- ◆ Enter dates into the Date Created or Date Saved frames to restrict the search to files created or saved within a certain range of dates.

3. Click the Start Search button in the Search dialog box. Word searches for the files that match your specifications and then closes the Search box. Back in the Find File dialog box, the matching files are listed in the File Name box.

4. Select any file name in the list to preview the document in the Content box.

5. Optionally, click the Summary button to see the selected file's Summary Info box.

6. Click the Options button to change the order in which the files are listed or the type of information displayed about a selected file. In the Options dialog box, choose among the following alternatives:

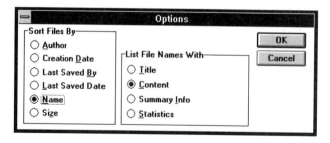

- ◆ In the Sort Files By box, select a sorting key for arranging the files. Word can sort the documents by file name (the default), author, date, or size.

- In the List File Names With box, select the type of information you want to view for the selected file. Word can display the document's content (the default), Summary Info box, Statistics box, or a table that includes file names and titles.

7. Click OK in the Options box. Word rearranges the elements of the Find File dialog box according to the options you have selected.

EXAMPLE

To review an example of the Find File dialog box, examine Figure 2.2 in Lesson 2.

NOTE

You can also open the Find File dialog box by clicking the Open button in the Toolbar and then clicking the Find File button in the Open dialog box.

TO OPEN, PRINT, DELETE, OR COPY ONE OR MORE FILES

1. Choose File ➤ Find File.

2. Click the Search button and define the file search, as described in the steps above.

3. In the resulting list of file names, select one or more files. To select multiple files, hold down the Ctrl key while you click additional file names in the list.

4. Select one of the following buttons at the bottom of the Find File dialog box:

- Click Open to open as many as nine selected files at once.
- Click Delete to delete the selected files. (Word displays a dialog box asking you to confirm the deletion.)
- Click Print to print all of the selected files in one operation.
- Click Copy to copy the selected files to a new location on disk. In the resulting Copy dialog box, select the directory path to which you want to copy the files, then click OK.

5. Click the Close button to close the Find File dialog box.

SEE ALSO

Deleting a Document from Disk, Opening a File, Previewing, Printing

FINDING TEXT AND STYLES

Using the Find command, you can search for occurrences of specific text entries and formatting in the current document.

TO FIND TEXT

1. Press Ctrl-Home if you want to search from the beginning of the current document, or Ctrl-End if you want to search from the end.

2. Choose Edit ➤ Find. The Find dialog box appears on the screen. Enter the text that you want to search for in the Find What text box.

3. Optionally, activate the Match Whole Word Only option if you want to search for whole word occurrences rather than letters embedded within a word. Activate the Match Case option if you want Word to search for text in the exact uppercase/lowercase pattern you have entered into the Find What box.

4. Select Up or Down in the Direction box to specify the direction of the search. (Down is the default.)

5. Click the Find Next button to search for the text. If the text is found, Word scrolls to its location in your document and selects it. The Find dialog box remains on the screen. Click Find Next again to find the next occurrence.

6. Click Cancel to close the Find dialog box.

Shortcut: To repeat the previous Find operation after closing the Find dialog box, press Shift-F4. Word retains the information you previously entered into the Find dialog box and performs the search exactly as before.

NOTE

In the Find What text box you can use the question mark (?) to represent an unspecified character. In addition, you can use the caret symbol (^) along with a letter to represent certain special characters; for example, ^t represents a tab character, and ^p a paragraph mark.

TO FIND FORMATTING OR FORMATTED TEXT

1. Choose Edit ➤ Find.
2. If you want to search for a format pattern without specifying a particular text sequence, delete the contents of the Find What text box (or leave the box empty). On the other hand, if you want to search for a combination of text and formatting, enter the text into the Find What box.
3. Select settings for the Match Whole Word Only, Match Case, and Direction options.
4. Click one or all of the Character, Paragraph, or Styles buttons, in any order. In the resulting dialog boxes, select the formatting patterns that you want to search for. A description of the current formatting search pattern appears just beneath the Find What text box.
5. Click the Find Next button to search for the format pattern or the formatted text.

Shortcut: In the Find dialog box, you can use familiar keyboard shortcuts to specify formatting (instead of clicking the Character or Paragraph buttons). For example, press Ctrl-B, Ctrl-I, or Ctrl-U to search for bold, italics or underlining; and Ctrl-L for left-alignment, Ctrl-E for Centering, Ctrl-R for right-alignment, or Ctrl-J for justification.

EXAMPLE

To find all bold occurrences of the name *Lantern* in the current document, choose Edit ➤ Find and enter **Lantern** into the Find What text box. Press Ctrl-B to specify the bold format, then activate the Match Case option. Click the Find Next button multiple times until you see the message "Word has reached the end of the document."

NOTE

Click the Clear button to clear any formatting patterns from the Find dialog box.

SEE ALSO

Formatting Paragraphs, Formatting Text, Replacing Text and Styles, Styles

FONTS

In Word you can select from the screen and printer fonts that are available in your installation of Windows.

TO CHANGE THE FONT IN A DOCUMENT

1. Choose Format ➤ Character. The Character dialog box appears on the screen.
2. Pull down the Font list and select the name of an available font.
3. Click OK.

Shortcut: Pull down the Font list in the ribbon and select a font from the list.

EXAMPLES

Here are some samples of fonts that may be available for your use:

Arial MT
Bodoni BoldCondensed
BrushScript
CG Times
Courier
DomCasual
Helvetica

LetterGothic
Line Printer
Modern
NewsGothic
Perpetua
Script
Univers

SEE ALSO

Formatting Text, Point Size

FOOTNOTES

Word simplifies the process of entering and managing footnotes. When you insert a footnote, Word creates a numbered *reference mark* in the main text of your document, and renumbers any other reference marks if necessary. If you move or delete a footnote reference mark, Word automatically makes the appropriate adjustments in the footnotes themselves.

TO INSERT A NUMBERED FOOTNOTE

1. Choose View ➤ Normal, if necessary, to switch to Normal view.

2. Move the insertion point to where you want the footnote reference mark to appear and choose Insert ➤ Footnote. In the Footnote dialog box, the default option is Auto-Numbered Footnote.

3. If you want to specify the location for your footnotes, click the Options button. In the Footnote Options dialog box, pull down the Place At list, and select a location: End of Section, Bottom of Page (the default), Beneath Text, or End of Document. Click OK to close the Footnote Options dialog box.

4. Click OK in the Footnote dialog box. Word inserts a numbered reference mark into your document and opens the Footnote pane at the bottom of the screen. The same reference mark appears at the beginning of the current line in the Footnote pane.

5. Type the text of your footnote, then click Close at the top of the Footnote pane.

6. Choose View ➤ Page Layout to see how your footnote will look on the printed page.

EXAMPLE

Here is an example of a short document with three footnotes:

> When you first start Word for Windows, you'll see an empty document window in which you can begin typing text. Above the document are three option bars:
>
> • The *Toolbar* contains a unique collection of *buttons* designed to streamline operations in Word.[1]
> • The *ribbon* displays options for changing the appearance of text in a document.[2]
> • The *ruler* gives you simple ways to control margins and tabs in the active document.[3]
>
> ---
>
> [1] To view a quick one-line description of any button in the Toolbar, position the mouse pointer over your selection and hold down the left mouse button.
>
> [2] To hide the ribbon from view, choose the Ribbon command from the View menu.
>
> [3] Each document window has its own ruler.

NOTES

If you prefer to use a symbol such as an asterisk as the footnote reference mark, choose the Custom Footnote Mark option in the Footnote dialog box, and enter the symbol in the corresponding text box.

Three buttons at the bottom of the Footnote Options dialog box allow you to revise special elements of the footnote presentation. Click the Separator button to change the separator line that appears between the text of your document and the footnotes. Click *Cont. Separator* to change the separator line for footnotes that continue from the previous page. Click *Cont. Notice* to enter a short piece of text—such as *Continued...* — for a long footnote that must be continued on the next page. When you click one of these buttons, Word opens a Footnote pane that displays the default.

TO MOVE A FOOTNOTE

Select the footnote reference mark and use the Cut and Paste buttons to move it to a new location. Word adjusts the footnotes themselves automatically.

TO DELETE A FOOTNOTE

Select the footnote reference mark and press Del. Again, Word makes the necessary adjustments in the footnotes themselves.

FORMATTING PAGES

The Page Setup command supplies options for controlling the appearance of your document on the printed page: margins, paper size, orientation, and paper source.

TO CHANGE THE PAGE SETTINGS

Choose Format ➤ Page Setup. At the top of the Page Setup dialog box are three option buttons, labeled Margins, Size and Orientation, and Paper Source. When you click one of these buttons, Word displays the corresponding set of options in the dialog box:

- The Margins options include text boxes for the four margins: Top, Bottom, Left, and Right. In addition, you can click the Facing Pages check box to arrange mirror-image pages for double-sided printing. Use the Gutter setting to provide extra space along the inside margin for binding a document.

- The Size and Orientation settings include paper size and the direction of text on the page. To establish the paper size, you can choose from the list of standard sizes in the Paper Size box, or you can enter specific numeric dimensions in the Width and Height boxes. The Orientation box has two options: Portrait prints each line of text horizontally across the width of the page. Landscape rotates the text by 90 degrees, printing each line vertically across the length of the page.

- ◆ The Paper Source options include a list of paper trays for the first page and another list for the remaining pages of your document.

As you make changes in these settings, the Sample box shows the effect on the printed page. You can pull down the Apply To list and specify how you want to apply the page formatting—for example, to the whole document or only to the current section. Click the Use as Default button to incorporate these new settings into the current template.

Shortcut: You can change a document's left and right margins by clicking the margin-scale symbol on the ruler and then sliding the margin markers to new positions.

SEE ALSO

Margins, Page Orientations, Printing, Templates

FORMATTING PARAGRAPHS

The Paragraph command supplies options for formatting a paragraph: alignment, indentation, spacing, and page breaks.

TO CHANGE THE PARAGRAPH SETTINGS

Move the insertion point into the paragraph you want to format and choose Format ➤ Paragraph. Make selections and entries in the Paragraph dialog box:

- ◆ Choose Left, Centered, Right, or Justified from the Alignment list.

- ◆ Change the measurements in the indentation boxes: From Left and From Right for the entire paragraph's left and right indents, and First Line for the position of the top line.

- ◆ Enter line spacing values in the Spacing text boxes: Before and After to change the spacing between the current paragraph and the text that comes before and after it; and Line Spacing for the spacing within the paragraph. The Line Spacing list contains standard settings such as Single and Double.

- Select Pagination options to insert a page break before the paragraph (Page Break); to print the current paragraph and the next paragraph on the same page (Keep With Next); and to keep the entire current paragraph on one page (Keep Lines Together).

As you make changes in these settings, the Sample box shows how the paragraph will appear on the page.

Shortcuts: Click buttons on the ribbon to change the alignment of the current paragraph. Use the ruler to adjust indentations. Press Ctrl-1, Ctrl-2, or Ctrl-5 for single, double, or 1½-line spacing in a paragraph. Press Ctrl-↵ to insert a hard page break.

SEE ALSO

Aligning, Hanging Indents, Indenting, Page Breaks, Spacing between Lines, Widows and Orphans

FORMATTING TEXT

The Character command supplies options for changing the appearance of a selection of text: font, point size, style, color, superscript or subscript, and spacing between characters.

TO CHANGE THE FORMAT OF A TEXT SELECTION

Select the text and choose Format ➤ Character. Make selections in the Character dialog box:

- Select a font, point size, and color from the Font, Points, and Color lists.

- Select any combination of styles from the Style box: Bold, Italic, Strikethrough, Hidden, Small Caps, All Caps. Choose an underline style in the Underline list: None, Single, Words Only, or Double.

- In the Super/subscript list, select None, Superscript, or Subscript. Optionally, enter a point measurement in the corresponding By box for the amount of offset.

- In the Spacing list, select Normal, Expanded, or Condensed to change the amount of space between characters. Optionally, enter a point measurement in the corresponding By box.

As you make changes in these settings, the Sample box shows how the text will appear. Click the Use as Default button to incorporate these new settings into the current template.

Shortcuts: Click the Bold, Italics, or Underline buttons on the ribbon to change the style of a selection, and use the Font and Point boxes to choose a font and a point size.

SEE ALSO

Colors, Fonts, Point Size, Styles, Spacing between Characters, Subscripts and Superscripts, Templates

FRAMES

A frame is a movable box of text or graphics. You can insert a frame around existing text or graphics in a document or you can create an empty frame and then insert contents into the frame. By default, any other text in your document wraps around the frame. After creating a frame, you can use the mouse or the Format ➤ Frame command to position and resize the frame and to establish other characteristics.

TO CREATE, MOVE, AND RESIZE A FRAME FOR EXISTING TEXT OR GRAPHICS

1. Select the text or graphics that are to become the contents of the frame and choose Insert ➤ Frame. Word displays a single-line border and handles around the perimeter of the frame.

2. To move the frame, position the mouse pointer over the frame's border; the pointer becomes a four-headed arrow icon. Drag the frame to any new position in your document.

3. To resize the frame, position the mouse pointer over one of the six handles arranged around the perimeter. The pointer becomes a two-headed arrow icon, pointing vertically, horizontally, or diagonally. Drag the pointer to decrease or increase the size. When you release the mouse button, Word rearranges the contents inside the frame.

Shortcut: To create a frame, select the text or graphics that are to become the frame's contents and click the Frame button on the Toolbar.

EXAMPLE

For an example of a frame, turn back to *Lesson 5* and examine Figures 5.1 and 5.8.

NOTE

You can change the style of the border around a frame by clicking the frame's current border (to select the frame) and choosing Format ➤ Border.

TO CHANGE THE MEASUREMENTS AND APPEARANCE OF A FRAME

Click the frame's border to select the frame, then choose Format ➤ Frame. In the Frame dialog box make any of the following changes:

- To control the arrangement of the text around the frame, choose None or Around in the Text Wrapping box.

- In the Size box, enter new measurements for the width and height of the frame.

- In the Horizontal and Vertical boxes, enter new measurements or options for the frame's position in relation to the page, the margins, a column, or a paragraph. You can also enter measurements for the horizontal and vertical distance from the frame to the text around the frame.

TO CREATE AN EMPTY FRAME

Deselect any text or graphics and click the Frame button. The mouse pointer becomes a cross hair. Drag the mouse to specify the desired size and position of the frame.

TO REMOVE A FRAME

1. Click the frame's border to select the frame.
2. Choose Format ➤ Frame and click the Remove Frame button. Word inserts the frame's contents into the text of the document.
3. Optionally, choose Format ➤ Border and click None in the Preset box. Then click OK to remove the border around the contents of the former frame.

TO DELETE A FRAME AND ITS CONTENTS

Select the frame and press Del.

SEE ALSO

Borders, Columns, Margins

GLOSSARY ENTRIES

A glossary entry is an item of text or a graphic (or a combination of both) that you use frequently in documents. Once you assign this entry a name and add it to the glossary, you can quickly insert the entry into a document just by typing a few keystrokes.

TO CREATE A NEW GLOSSARY ENTRY

1. In the current document, select the text or graphics that you want to add to the glossary, then choose Edit ➤ Glossary.

2. In the Glossary Name box, enter a name for the new glossary entry, then click the Define button. This closes the Glossary dialog box and adds your entry to the glossary.

3. If the current document is based on a template other than NORMAL.DOT, Word may display a new dialog box asking you where you want to store the glossary. Click the As Global option to store the glossary entry globally, for use in any document; or click the In Template option to store the entry for use only in documents based on the current template.

NOTE

To specify the destination for future glossary entries, choose File ➤ Template and select one of the options in the box labeled Store New Macros and Glossaries As. The three options are Global, With Document Template, or Prompt for Each New (the default).

TO INSERT THE CONTENTS OF A GLOSSARY ENTRY INTO A DOCUMENT

1. Move the insertion point to the position where you want to insert the entry and choose Edit ➤ Glossary. The Glossary dialog box lists the names of all available glossary entries.

2. Select a glossary name from the list and click the Insert button. The contents of the entry appear in your document.

Shortcut: Type the name of a glossary entry into your document and press F3. Word replaces the name you have typed with the contents of the glossary entry.

EXAMPLE

To insert a glossary entry named *logo* into your document, type **logo** at the position where you want the entry, and press F3.

SEE ALSO

Spike, Templates

GO TO

Using the Go To command, you can jump to a page location, section, line, bookmark, footnote, or annotation in your document.

TO GO TO A NEW LOCATION

Choose Edit ➤ Goto and enter one of the following in the Go To text box:

- ◆ A page number.
- ◆ A plus or minus sign followed by an integer. (The insertion point moves the number of pages forward or backward from the current position.)
- ◆ The letter *s* followed by a section number, or *l* followed by a line number.
- ◆ A bookmark name. (Or select a name from the list of bookmarks beneath the Go To text box.)
- ◆ The letter *f* followed by a footnote number or the letter *a* followed by an annotation number. (The insertion point jumps to the footnote reference mark or to the annotation mark.)
- ◆ A number followed by a percent sign (%). (The insertion point jumps through a percentage of the document relative to the beginning.)

Shortcut: Press F5 and enter the destination after the prompt in the status bar. (Press F5 twice or double-click the status bar to open the Go To dialog box.)

NOTE

After a jump, press Shift-F5 to return to the previous location.

G

SEE ALSO

Annotations, Bookmarks, Footnotes, Sections

GRAMMAR CHECKS

The Grammar command reviews all or part of your document for possible grammatical errors.

TO CHECK THE GRAMMAR OF A DOCUMENT

1. Select the sentence, paragraph, or portion of the document you want to check; or deselect any text to check the entire document.

2. Choose Tools ➤ Grammar. Word begins checking your document. In the Grammar dialog box Word displays possible errors in the Sentence box, along with explanations or possible corrections in the Suggestions box. You can choose to change the sentence, ignore the suggestion, or request a more detailed explanation. When the grammar check is complete, Word displays the Readability Statistics box, providing a variety of information about the writing style in your document.

EXAMPLE

Figures 4.6, 4.7, and 4.8 in *Lesson 4* illustrate the Grammar dialog boxes.

NOTE

To change the operation of the Grammar command, choose Tools ➤ Options and click the Grammar icon in the Category list (or click the Options button in the Grammar dialog box). In the Options box you can choose among three modes of grammar checking (Strictly, For Business Writing, For Casual Writing). To view specific lists of grammar rules—and to select among them—click the Customize Settings button.

SEE ALSO

Spelling Checks, Thesaurus

GRAPH

In the Graph program you can create a variety of charts from tables of numeric data. The resulting graphic is inserted into your document as an *embedded object*.

TO CREATE A CHART IN MICROSOFT GRAPH

1. Select all or part of a table of data in your document.

2. Choose Insert ➤ Object. In the Object Type list, choose Microsoft Graph and then click OK. After a few seconds the Graph application window appears. Data from your document is copied to the application's Datasheet window. The Chart window shows an initial bar chart for the data.

3. Use the menu options in the Graph program to change the content and appearance of the chart.

4. When you have completed your work on the chart, choose File ➤ Exit and Return from the Graph program's menu bar. A dialog box asks you whether you want to update your Word document. Click Yes.

Shortcut: Select a table of data in your document and click the Graph button in the Toolbar to start Microsoft Graph.

EXAMPLE

For examples of charts created in Microsoft Graph, see Figures 7.1, 7.4, 7.5, and 7.6 in *Lesson 7*.

NOTE

You can use the Graph program's Datasheet window to develop a table of data for creating a chart. To do so, click the Graph button without making a selection in the document.

TO CHANGE THE SIZE AND SHAPE OF A CHART OBJECT

1. Click the object to select it. Word encloses the chart in a border with sizing handles.

2. Drag any one of the sizing handles to increase or decrease the size of the frame.

TO EDIT A CHART

Double-click the chart. This restarts the Graph program and copies the chart back into the program's Chart window.

SEE ALSO

Embedded Objects, Frames, Tables

HANGING INDENTS

In a hanging indent, the first line of a paragraph begins further to the left than the remaining lines. Word automatically creates hanging indents for paragraphs in bulleted and numbered lists.

TO CREATE A HANGING INDENT

1. Move the insertion point into the paragraph where you want to create the indent or select two or more paragraphs.
2. Choose Format ➤ Paragraph.
3. In the From Left text box, enter an indent measurement for the paragraph.
4. In the First Line box, enter a negative number representing a backward measurement from the paragraph's indent. Click OK.

Shortcut: In the ruler, drag both left-indent markers to the right, to establish the paragraph indent; then hold down Shift and drag the upper indent marker to the left, to establish the first-line indent. To establish the hanging indent for a bulleted list or numbered list, simply select the paragraphs and click the Bulleted List or Numbered List button in the Toolbar.

EXAMPLES

Here are examples of hanging indents:

This paragraph is indented one-half inch from the left margin, but the first line is indented back by one-half inch from the rest of the paragraph. The result is a hanging indent.

- In a bulleted or numbered paragraph, Word automatically creates a hanging indent. The first line is indented one-fourth inch back from the remaining lines.

SEE ALSO

Bulleted Lists, Formatting Paragraphs, Indenting, Numbered Lists

HEADERS AND FOOTERS

Headers and footers are lines of text that Word prints on each page of a document or a section. You can use a header or a footer to display a variety of information, such as the page number, the date, the title of your document, or your company name. In a document that is divided into multiple sections, you can define individual headers and footers for each section. Word also allows you to create different headers or footers for odd and even pages, and for the first page in a document or section.

TO CREATE A HEADER OR A FOOTER

1. If your document is divided into sections, move the insertion point to the section in which you want to create the header or footer.

2. Choose View ➤ Normal, then choose View ➤ Header/Footer. (You can create headers and footers in Page Layout view, but Word displays header and footer panes only in the Normal view.) The Header/Footer box initially lists two options: Header and Footer.

3. Click the Different First Page option if you want to create a different header or footer for the first page. Word adds First Header and First Footer entries to the Header/Footer list.

4. Click the Different Odd and Even Pages option if you want to create different headers or footers for odd and even pages. Word changes the Header/Footer list to Even Header, Even Footer, Odd Header, and Odd Footer.

5. Select the name of the header or footer you want to create and click OK. Word opens a header or footer pane.

6. Type the text of the header or footer inside the pane. Optionally, click the Page Number, Date, or Time buttons to add fields for these items into the header or footer. Use buttons on the ribbon to select character styles or paragraph alignments for the text.

7. Click the Close button to close the header or footer pane. Then choose View ➤ Page Layout to see how the header or footer will appear on the printed page.

EXAMPLE

See Figures 5.1 to 5.4 in *Lesson 5* to view an example of a footer.

NOTE

You can select from a variety of page-number styles by clicking the Page Numbers button in the Header/Footer dialog box.

SEE ALSO

Formatting Pages, Page Numbers, Sections

HELP

Like other major Windows applications, Word comes with an elaborate cross-referenced help system. Along with a complete selection of help topics, the system includes two tutorial programs and a special help feature for previous WordPerfect users.

TO GET HELP

Choose one of these features:

- ◆ Help ➤ Help Index provides general entry points into the help system.
- ◆ Help ➤ Getting Started and Help ➤ Learning Word are the on-line tutorial programs.
- ◆ Help ➤ WordPerfect Help is designed to introduce Word procedures to WordPerfect users.
- ◆ Help ➤ About displays a dialog box that shows the Word version number, the name of the registered user, and information about your system.

Shortcuts: Press Shift-F1 to change the mouse pointer to a help icon, then click any element in the Word window to select a particular help topic. For context-sensitive help, press F1 during any operation to get help about your current activity.

EXAMPLE

See Figure 1.4 in *Lesson 1* for an example of the Word Help window.

NOTE

Cross-reference topics are underlined in the Help window. To switch to a related topic, click any underlined word. To view a definition, click any word with dotted underlining.

HIDING TEXT

If you want a selection to be removed from view in the document window, you can format it as *hidden text*.

TO HIDE A SELECTION OF TEXT OR GRAPHICS

1. Select the text or graphics that you want to hide and choose Format ➤ Character.

2. In the Style box, click the Hidden option, then click OK.

Shortcut: Select the text or graphics that you want to format as hidden, then press Ctrl-H.

TO VIEW HIDDEN TEXT

Click the Show/Hide ¶ button on the ribbon. Word displays the hidden text with dotted underlining.

NOTE

Another way to view hidden text is to choose Tools ➤ Options, click the View icon in the Category list, and then click the Hidden Text option in the Nonprinting Characters box.

SEE ALSO

Formatting Text

HYPHENATING

Using the Hyphenation command, you can instruct Word to insert *optional hyphens* into selected words of a document. In unjustified text, hyphenation tends to produce more even line endings along the right margin. In justified text, hyphenation tends to reduce the loose appearance of the paragraph. The amount of hyphenation depends on the size you assign to the *hot zone*, an unmarked column at the right side of your document.

TO HYPHENATE A SELECTION OF TEXT

1. Select the paragraphs that you want to hyphenate and choose Tools ➤ Hyphenation.

2. In the Hyphenation dialog box, remove the X from the Hyphenate CAPS check box if you do not want uppercase words to be hyphenated.

3. Remove the X from the Confirm check box if you do not want to confirm each hyphenation as Word goes through the selection of text.

4. Optionally, change the Hot Zone measurement. A line's ending position in relation to the hot zone determines hyphenation. A small hot zone maximizes the effect of hyphenation, but may result in more hyphens than you want to see in a paragraph.

5. Click OK. If you have checked the Confirm option, Word displays each potential hyphenation in the Hyphenate At box. Click Yes to accept the word break or No to reject it. (You can also change the word break in the Hyphenate At box.) Word displays a message when the hyphenation process is complete.

Shortcuts: As you type a paragraph of text, you can press Ctrl-Hyphen to insert an optional hyphen within a word, or Ctrl-Shift-Hyphen to insert a nonbreaking hyphen.

EXAMPLE

The following example shows hyphenated and unhyphenated versions of the same justified paragraph:

> In unjustified text, Word's Hyphenation command can produce more even line endings along the right margin. In justified text, hyphenation tends to reduce the looseness of the paragraph. The amount of hyphenation depends on the size of the *hot zone*, an unmarked column at the right side of a document.

> In unjustified text, Word's Hyphenation command can produce more even line endings along the right margin. In justified text, hyphenation tends to reduce the looseness of the paragraph. The amount of hyphenation depends on the size of the *hot zone*, an unmarked column at the right side of a document.

Notice that there is less space between the words in the hyphenated paragraph on the right.

NOTE

When you edit or reformat a hyphenated paragraph, optional hyphens disappear from view if they are no longer needed. (You can view optional hyphens by clicking

the Show/Hide ¶ button on the ribbon.) By contrast, a word in which you have entered a nonbreaking hyphen is never split between lines.

SEE ALSO

Formatting Paragraphs, Special Characters

INDENTING

By indenting a selected paragraph you can display the text within narrower or wider boundaries than the rest of the document. You can use either the Paragraph command or the ruler to establish indents.

TO APPLY INDENT SETTINGS TO A PARAGRAPH

1. Move the insertion point into the paragraph or select all the paragraphs that you want to indent.

2. Choose Format ➤ Paragraph and change the settings in the From Right, From Left, and First Line boxes. As you make these changes, the result is depicted in the Sample box.

3. Click OK.

Shortcut: Drag the indent markers to new positions in the ruler. To move the first-line indent marker independently, hold down the Shift key while you drag.

SEE ALSO

Formatting Paragraphs, Hanging Indents, Ruler, Tabs

INDEXING

Word vastly simplifies creating an index for a document. To prepare for an index, you use the Index Entry command to insert index-entry fields at appropriate locations in your document. You can create primary entries along with subentries. Then you use the Index command to create the index itself. Word does all the work of compiling the entries, inserting the page numbers, and alphabetizing the index.

TO INSERT AN INDEX ENTRY FIELD

1. Select a sequence of text (up to 64 characters) or move the insertion point to where you want to insert the index entry.

2. Choose Insert – Index Entry. In the Index Entry box you can enter or revise the text of the index entry. You can also specify a range of pages for the entry by selecting a bookmark name in the Range list. (This step assumes that you have already defined the appropriate bookmark in your document.)

3. Click Bold or Italic to apply a format to the entry's page number. Then click OK. Word inserts an index entry field (named XE) at the current location in your document.

NOTES

To view hidden index entry fields, click the Show/Hide ¶ button in the ribbon.

To define an index subentry, enter the name of the main entry, followed by a colon, and then the name of the subentry. For example, **West African Writers:Sembene, Ousmane** creates the main entry *West African Writers* and the subentry *Sembene, Ousmane*.

TO CREATE AN INDEX

1. Insert as many index-entry fields in your document as necessary.

2. Move the insertion point to the location where you want to place the index, and choose Insert ➤ Index.

3. In the Index dialog box, choose between the Normal Index and Run-in Index options. In a normal index, Word indents subentries on a separate line after a main entry. In a run-in index, subentries are separated from the main entry by semicolons.

4. In the Heading Separator box, choose an option for the visual separator between letter sections in the index: None, Blank Line, or Letter. (The Letter option actually inserts a letter—A, B, C, and so on—at the top of each section.)

5. Click OK. Word compiles and sorts the index and inserts an INDEX field at the current location in your document. The result of this field is the index itself.

6. If you wish, apply formatting to the index list; for example, you might want to display it in multiple newspaper-style columns.

EXAMPLE

Here is an example of a short index, created from an expanded version of the bookstore newsletter (presented in *Lessons 4, 5,* and 6):

A	fiction, 1, 4	**N**
After Good-bye, 5	foreign publishers, 2	Neighborhood Readers Forum, 3, 4
Authors	foreign-language books, 2-3	Nelson, John, 5
Deller, James, 5	French language books, 2	*New Russia, The, 5*
Madsen, Willa, 4		*New York Times Book Review,* 1
Maxton, Freida, 5	**G**	
Nelson, John, 5	German, 3	**P**
Sembene, Ousmane, 2	Greek, 3	paperbacks, 1
Tanner, Pat, 5		
Weinberg, Ella, 5	**H**	**R**
	Hall, Jane, 4	reading area, 1-2
B	hard cover books, 1	reference section, 1
book bags, 1	*Heart of San Francisco, 4*	Russian, 3
	Home from the Moon, 5	
C		**S**
Californians and the National	**I**	Sembene, Ousmane, 2, 4
Election, 3	Italian, 3	Spanish, 3
Cantonese, 3		
children's books, 1, 3	**J**	**T**
	Japanese, 3	Tanner, Pat, 5
D		*The 1992 Election Year Handbook, 3*
Deller, James, 5	**L**	
Dutch, 3	*Le Mandat, 2, 4*	**W**
	film, 4	Weinberg, Ella, 5
E	*Les bouts de bois de Dieu, 2*	West African writers, 2
election books, 3		Sembene, Ousmane, 2, 4
	M	*When in Paris, 5*
F	Madsen, Willa, 4	
Feeling Smart, 5	Maxton, Freida, 5	

Notice the use of both primary entries and subentries. You'll also find an example of a page range, defined by a bookmark entry in the document.

SEE ALSO

Bookmarks, Fields, Table of Contents

INSERTING A FILE

You can use the Insert ➤ File command to insert all or part of the contents of a file into the current document.

TO INSERT TEXT OR GRAPHICS FROM A FILE ON DISK

1. In the current document, move the insertion point to where you want to insert the file.

2. Choose Insert ➤ File.

3. Use the Directories and Drives boxes to find the path location of the source file, then select the file from the File Name list or enter the name directly into the File Name text box.

4. If you want to insert only a part of the source file, enter a bookmark name into the Range text box. (This step assumes that you have previously defined this bookmark in the source file.)

5. Click OK. Word copies the entire file or the portion of the file identified by the bookmark into the current document.

SEE ALSO

Bookmarks, Links

LANGUAGES

You can use the Language command to identify selections of text written in foreign languages. Then when you choose the Spelling, Grammar, Thesaurus, and Hyphenation commands, Word uses the appropriate foreign-language dictionary—if it is available—to check the passages. (To use this feature, you must purchase and install the necessary foreign-language proofing tools.)

TO MARK THE LANGUAGE OF A SELECTION

1. Select the foreign-language passage in your document, and choose Format ➤ Language.

2. In the Language dialog box, select the correct language from the list labeled Mark Selected Text As. Then click OK.

NOTE

If you do not have the necessary proofing tools for a foreign language—or if you simply want Word to skip a selected passage of text during proofing procedures—choose the *(no proofing)* option from the top of the Mark Selected Text As list. Accordingly, the Spelling, Grammar, and Hyphenation tools ignore the marked selection of text.

SEE ALSO

Grammar Checks, Hyphenation, Spelling Checks, Thesaurus

LINKS

You can establish a *link*—a means of data exchange—between a Word document and a selection of text or data in another Windows document. The *source* can be a Word document file or a file created in another Windows application—for example, an Excel worksheet. Whenever changes take place in the text or data of the source file, Word can update the link in the destination document.

TO CREATE A LINK
BETWEEN TWO WORD DOCUMENTS

1. Open the source document and define a bookmark for the selection of text or graphics that is to be the object of the link. Then save and close the source document.

2. Open the destination document and move the insertion point to the location where you want to insert the link.

3. Choose Insert ➤ File. Enter the name of the source file in the File Name text box. (Use the Directories and Drives boxes, if necessary, to identify the file's path.)

4. In the Range text box enter the bookmark name you defined in the source file.

5. Click the Link to File option to place an X in the corresponding check box. Then click OK. Word inserts an INCLUDE field in the destination document to represent the linked selection from the source document.

EXAMPLE

The INCLUDE field identifies the source file and the bookmark representing the linked text or graphics. For example, here is the INCLUDE field for a bookmark named MARKER in a file named SOURCE.DOC:

    {INCLUDE C:\\SOURCE.DOC MARKER}

NOTES

When there is a change in the source document, you can update the destination document by moving the insertion point into the INCLUDE field and pressing F9. (Press Shift-F9 to toggle between field codes and the field result.)

To link an entire source document to a destination document, leave the Range box empty in the File dialog box.

TO CREATE A LINK WITH A SOURCE
DOCUMENT FROM ANOTHER APPLICATION

1. Open the source file in the second application and select the data that will be the object of the link. For example, select a range of cells in an Excel

worksheet. Then choose the application's Edit ➤ Copy command to copy the selection to the Clipboard.

2. Open the destination document in Word and move the insertion point to the location where you want to paste the link.

3. Choose Word's Edit ➤ Paste Special command. In the Data Type box, select an appropriate option for the data you are linking—for example, Formatted Text for a range selection in an Excel worksheet.

4. Click the Paste Link button. Word inserts a LINK field in the destination document to represent the source of the data.

EXAMPLE

Here is the LINK field for a range of cells in an Excel worksheet named SOURCE.XLS:

{LINK ExcelWorksheet C:\\SOURCE.XLS R1C1:R5C2 \ * mergeformat \r \a}

Notice that the LINK field gives three items of information about the source: the application, the document, and the range of data.

NOTE

A LINK field can be updated automatically or manually. To switch between these two options, choose Edit ➤ Link (available only when the current document contains one or more links) and click the Automatic or Manual option.

SEE ALSO

Embedded Objects, Inserting a File

LOCKING A DOCUMENT

You can *lock* a file to prevent other users from editing the text. Other users are still allowed to insert annotations in a locked file.

TO LOCK A FILE

1. Choose File ➤ Save As and click the File Sharing button.

2. In the File Sharing dialog box, click the Lock File for Annotations option to place an X in the corresponding check box.

3. Optionally, enter a password into the Password text box. (Word prompts you to enter the password twice; each entry appears as a string of asterisks in the Password box.)

4. Click the OK buttons on the File Sharing and Save As dialog boxes.

SEE ALSO

Opening a File, Saving

MACROS

Macros are shortcuts for accomplishing everyday tasks in Word. Each macro is a recorded sequence of instructions for performing a procedure. You choose the Record Macro command to create a macro and assign it a shortcut key; then whenever you press the key combination, Word performs your macro. To make a macro even more accessible, you can use the Options command to create a new button on the toolbar for the macro.

TO RECORD A MACRO

1. Choose Tools ➤ Record Macro.
2. Enter a name for your macro in the Record Macro Name text box.
3. Optionally, select a shortcut key in the Key text box. (If the key you select is already assigned to another macro, the name of that macro appears next to the Currently label in the Shortcut Key box.) By default, an X appears in both the Ctrl and Shift check boxes, resulting in a shortcut combination of Ctrl-Shift-*key*.
4. Optionally, enter a brief description of this new macro in the Description text box.
5. Click OK to begin recording the macro. (If the current document is based on a template other than NORMAL.DOT, Word displays a dialog box asking you where you want to store the macro; click *as Global* or *in Template*.) The notation *REC* appears in the status bar, indicating that Word is ready to record your macro.
6. Perform the sequence of commands and actions that you want to record in the macro. (While you are recording, use the keyboard rather than the mouse to perform any text operations inside your document.)
7. When you have finished the sequence of actions, choose Tools ➤ Stop Recorder.

EXAMPLE

One simple use for macros is to produce characters that normally require a code entry on the numeric keypad—including the em dash and the "curled" quotation marks. (See *Dashes* and *Quotation Marks* for information about these characters.) For example, to create a macro for the em dash, choose Tools ➤ Record Macro, enter **EmDash** as the macro name, select Ctrl-Shift-**M** as the shortcut key, and click OK. When *REC* appears on the status bar, activate the numeric keypad and press Alt-0150 on the keypad. Choose Tools ➤ Stop Recorder to complete the recording. Now you can press Ctrl-Shift-M to type an em dash into a document.

NOTE

When you choose File ➤ Exit after creating one or more global macros, Word asks you whether you want to update the global changes. Click Yes to save your macros for future sessions with Word. To save a macro before exiting Word, choose File ➤ Save All.

TO CREATE A BUTTON ON THE TOOLBAR FOR A MACRO

1. Choose Tools ➤ Options. In the Options dialog box, click the Toolbar icon in the Categories list.

2. In the Show box, click Macros to see a list of macros you have installed yourself, or Commands to see a list of Word's built-in macro commands.

3. Select a macro name in the Macros list, and a button for the macro in the Button list. Pull down the Tool to Change list, and select the current Toolbar button (or space) that you want to replace with the new button.

4. Click Change, then click Close to close the dialog box. The new button appears in the Toolbar. Try performing your macro by clicking the new button.

EXAMPLE

A new button has been added to the right end of this Toolbar to represent the EmDash macro:

NOTE

You can also use the Options command to create a new menu command for a macro: Choose Tools ➤ Options and click the Menu icon in the Categories list. Make selections in the Menu and Macros lists and click Add.

TO RUN, EDIT, RENAME, OR DELETE A MACRO

Choose Tools ➤ Macro, select a macro from the Macro Name list, and click the Run, Edit, Rename, or Delete button.

NOTE

When you click the Edit button in the Macro dialog box, Word displays the macro editing window. You can revise or expand your macro, using the statements and functions of the WordBasic programming language.

SEE ALSO

Templates, Toolbar

MAILING LABELS

To produce mailing labels in Word you use a specialized *print merge* procedure. Like all print merges, mailing labels require a *main document* and a *data file*. (See *Print Merge* and *Tables* for details.) Because the main document for mailing labels needs some special elements, Word supplies a template that creates the main document for you. The template is named MAILLABL.DOT; when you open a new document based on this template, an automatic macro begins guiding you through the process of creating your mailing labels. You can apply this process to a mailing-list data file that you have previously created and saved on disk or you can create a new data file.

TO PRINT MAILING LABELS
FROM AN EXISTING DATA FILE

1. Choose File ➤ New. In the Use Template list, select MAILLABL.
2. Click OK. Word opens a new document based on MAILLABL.DOT and begins running the automatic macro that is stored in the template. The macro displays a series of dialog boxes asking you for instructions.
3. In the first dialog box, select a mailing-label sheet format from the Product Number List. (These product numbers correspond to a variety of standard label forms.) Word inserts an empty table into the new document and formats the rows and columns to match the sheet format you have selected.

4. The next dialog box gives you a choice between printing a single label or multiple labels. Click the Multiple Label button to perform a print-merge operation with your address file.

5. Next a dialog box asks you how your address list is organized—as two files (a header file for the field names and a data file for the addresses) or as a single file (a data table that includes its own field names). Click the No button if you have stored the field names and data table together in one file.

6. The Attach Data File dialog box appears on the next screen. In the File Name list, select the name of your address data file. Then click OK. (If you have not yet created an address-list data file, click the Create Data File button; Word guides you through the process of creating the file.)

7. Word displays a new dialog box titled Layout Mailing Labels. Use the controls in this box to design your labels: To insert a merge field name into the label, click the field in the Field Names list, then click the Add to Label button. To insert a space, comma, period, or new line, select the appropriate entry in the Special Characters list, then click Add to Label. The layout appears in the Sample Mailing Label box.

8. Click the Done button when you are finished with the layout. Word inserts the layout you have designed into each cell of the table in the main document. Then a final dialog box describes the steps you can take next. Click OK to continue.

9. In the print-merge bar, click the Merge to Printer button to begin printing your labels.

NOTE

You can create a main document for mailing labels without using the MAIL-LABL.DOT template: Insert a table into an empty document and resize the rows and columns to imitate a single page of the label sheet you plan to use. Choose File ➤ Print Merge and attach your address data file to the document. In the first cell of the table in the main document, insert merge field names to create the layout for your labels; then copy this layout to each cell in the table. Finally, insert a NEXT field at the beginning of all but the first cell in the table. (During the print-merge procedure, {NEXT} instructs Word to insert each individual address record into a new cell of the table.)

SEE ALSO

Fields, Print Merge, Tables, Templates

MARGINS

The top, bottom, left, right, and gutter margins determine the boundaries of the text on a printed page. You can use the Page Setup command, the ruler, or the Print Preview window to change the margins.

TO CHANGE THE MARGINS OF A DOCUMENT

1. Choose Format ➤ Page Setup. If necessary, click the Margins option button at the top of the Page Setup dialog box.

2. Adjust the measurements in the Top, Bottom, Left, and Right boxes. (If you want the margins on facing pages to mirror each other, click the Facing Pages option. The Left and Right boxes become Inside and Outside.)

3. Optionally, enter a value in the Gutter box to leave extra room for binding your document. Then click OK.

Shortcuts: On the ruler, click the margin-scale symbol if the margin scale is not already displayed. Then drag the left- and right-margin markers to new positions along the scale. Alternatively, choose File ➤ Print Preview and click the Margins button. Select a page and drag any of the margin handles to new positions. Click Margins again to see how the new margins affect the page layout.

NOTE

To display a block of text inside the left- or right-margin area, select the text and click the Frame button. Resize the width of the resulting frame so it will fit within the margin, and then drag the frame into the margin. (Optionally, choose Format ➤ Frame to resize and reposition the frame by measurements rather than by sight.) Choose Format ➤ Character to change the text formatting in the frame. Choose Format ➤ Border and click None to remove the border around the frame.

SEE ALSO

Formatting Pages, Frames, Indenting, Hanging Indents, Previewing, Ruler

MOVING TEXT

To move text from one place to another within a document—or from one document to another—you can click the Cut and Paste buttons, using the Clipboard as a temporary storage area.

TO MOVE TEXT

1. Select the text and click the Cut button on the Toolbar (or choose Edit ➤ Cut).

2. Move the insertion point to the destination of the move and click the Paste button (or choose Edit ➤ Paste).

Shortcut: To move a block of text within a document, select the text and then drag the selection to its new location.

SEE ALSO

Copying Text, Spike

NEW DOCUMENT

Using the New command, you can open a new document based on the default NORMAL.DOT template or on any other template of your choice.

TO OPEN A NEW DOCUMENT

1. Choose File ➤ New.

2. In the Use Template list, select the name of the template on which you want to base the new document. (Look in the Description box for a description of the template you select in the list.)

3. Click OK. Word opens a new document that contains the styles, formatting, and other elements of the template you have selected. New documents receive default names such as *Document1*, *Document2*, and so on.

NOTE

To open a new blank document based on NORMAL.DOT, click the New button on the Toolbar.

SEE ALSO

Opening a File, Saving, Templates

NORMAL VIEW

In Normal view, Word displays page breaks as single dotted lines and section breaks as double dotted lines. Entering text in Normal view is often more efficient than in Page Layout view.

TO SWITCH TO NORMAL VIEW

Choose View ➤ Normal.

NOTE

To view the header or footer pane, switch to Normal view before choosing the View ➤ Header/Footer command; but to see how the resulting header or footer will appear on the printed page, switch to Page Layout view.

SEE ALSO

Draft Mode, Outlining, Page Layout View

NUMBERED LISTS

In a numbered list, Word displays a number or letter at the beginning of each line or paragraph. By default, paragraphs in a numbered list are formatted with *hanging indents*. You can select from several styles of numbering or lettering for the list.

TO CREATE A NUMBERED LIST

1. Select the sequence of lines or paragraphs that you want to include in the list and then Choose Tools ➤ Bullets and Numbering.

2. At the top of the Bullets and Numbering dialog box, click the Numbered List option button if it is not already selected.

3. In the Number box, select a number (or letter) format and a separator character for the list. If necessary, enter a new starting value in the Start At box.

4. If you want a larger or smaller indent for paragraphs in the list, adjust the setting in the Hanging Indent By text box. (If you do not want the paragraphs in the list to be formatted as hanging indents, click the Hanging Indent By option to remove the X from the check box.) The Sample box shows a model of the numbered list you are creating.

5. Click OK.

Shortcut: Select the lines or paragraphs of the list and click the Numbered List button in the Toolbar. Word applies the list format currently selected in the Numbered List dialog box.

EXAMPLES

Here are examples of numbered lists formatted with and without hanging indents:

1. The paragraphs in this numbered list are formatted as hanging indents.
2. The first line of each paragraph appears further to the left than the remaining lines.
3. As a result, the numbers are aligned at the left of the paragraphs.

[I] The paragraphs in this list are not formatted as hanging indents.
[II] As a result, the numbers are aligned with the left margin of the text.
[III] Notice the selection of Roman numerals and bracket separators in this list.
[IV] These are among the options available in the Bullets and Numbering dialog box.

SEE ALSO

Bulleted Lists, Hanging Indents, Outlining

OPENING A FILE

You use the Open command to reopen documents that are stored on disk.

TO OPEN A DOCUMENT

Choose File ➤ Open. If necessary, use the Directories and Drives boxes to find the correct search path. Choose the name of the document from the File Name list or enter the name directly into the File Name text box. Then click OK.

Shortcuts: Click the Open button on the Toolbar to view the Open dialog box. Alternatively, to open one of the four files that you have used most recently, select the file name from the bottom of the File menu.

NOTE

Click Read Only in the Open dialog box if you want to open the document for reading but not revision.

SEE ALSO

Converting Document Formats, Finding a File

OPTIONS FOR WORD SETTINGS

The Options command gives you control over the way Word looks and operates. In the Options dialog box you can customize several categories of procedures and conditions in Word.

TO CHANGE AN OPTION

Choose Tools ➤ Options and click one of the icons in the Category list. When you do so, the Options dialog box displays options for the category you have selected:

- ◆ The View category contains check-box options that control the appearance of the application window and documents. For example, you can choose to hide or display the scroll bars and the status bar. You can also specify the width for the *styles area*, an optional display column at the left side of a document in Normal view. (The styles area identifies styles used in the paragraphs of a document. Because the width of this area is 0 by default, it is not visible unless you reset its width.) Finally, you can use the View category to establish the default display settings for elements of a document, including field codes and special characters that are normally hidden.

- In the General category you can toggle several Word features on or off. For example, you can activate or deactivate the drag-and-drop operation for moving text from one place to another in a document; and you can specify the function of the Ins key. (By default, Ins toggles the keyboard between insert and typeover modes, but you can instead use it to paste information from the Clipboard.) The General category also displays a list box labeled Measurement Units; from this list you can choose a default unit—inches, centimeters, points, or picas—for the ruler and for Word commands that display measurement boxes.

- The Print category displays options for printing documents. In particular, you can choose to print several kinds of information along with your document: summary information, field codes, annotations, and hidden text.

- The Save category controls saving options such as backups, summary-information prompts, and automatic saves.

- The Spelling and Grammar categories allow you to customize the operation of these two proofing tools.

- In the User Info category, you can change information about yourself and your address: In the three text boxes you can change the default Author name that Word enters into the Summary Info box, the initials used for annotations, and the return address that appears in the Create Envelope dialog box.

- In the Toolbar and Menus categories you can create new buttons and menu commands to represent macros you have installed in Word.

- The Keyboard category allows you to change the shortcut keys for existing macros.

- In the Win.ini category you can edit the WIN.INI startup files for Word.

Shortcut: To open the Options dialog box and select the Toolbar category, double-click any blank space within the Toolbar.

SEE ALSO

Annotations, Grammar Checks, Macros, Printing, Printing Envelopes, Ruler, Saving, Special Characters, Spelling Checks, Styles, Summary Information

OUTLINING

In Outline view you can develop the headings of an outline, and you can insert *body text* under any heading. Using the Outline bar, you can quickly reorganize your outline—promoting and demoting headings and body text, moving headings to new locations up or down the outline, and selecting a heading level for viewing. Finally, you can select a numbering scheme for your outline from the Bullets and Numbering dialog box.

TO CREATE AN OUTLINE

1. Choose View ➤ Outline. The Outline bar appears above your document.

2. Type a top-level heading. Word assigns the style named *heading 1* to this heading. Optionally, press ↵ and type additional top-level headings.

3. After any top-level heading, press ↵ and click the Demote button—the second button on the Outline bar—or press Alt-Shift-→ on the keyboard. This creates a second-level heading, to which Word assigns the style *heading 2*. By pressing the Demote button repeatedly, you can create as many as nine levels of headings in your outline, displayed in styles from *heading 1* to *heading 9*.

4. After any heading, click ↵ and press the Body Text button—the fifth button in the Outline bar—to create a text level. Type any amount of text beneath the heading.

EXAMPLE

Examine Figure 9.9 in *Lesson 9* for an example of an outline displayed in Outline view. Notice that Word displays two kinds of symbols before headings: A plus symbol appears next to a heading that contains subheadings or subtext, and a minus symbol appears next to a heading that does not. A small square appears next to paragraphs of body text in Outline view.

TO PROMOTE OR DEMOTE
THE LEVEL OF A HEADING

Move the insertion point to the heading you want to change, and click the Promote or Demote button—the first or second button on the Outline bar; or at the keyboard press Alt-Shift-← or Alt-Shift-→.

Shortcut: Drag any heading symbol horizontally to a new heading level. This changes the level of the heading and its subheadings.

TO MOVE A HEADING UP OR DOWN THE OUTLINE

Select a heading (optionally, along with its subheadings or subtext) and click the Up or Down button—the third and fourth buttons in the Outline bar; or, at the keyboard press Alt-Shift-↑ or Alt-Shift-↓.

Shortcut: Drag a heading symbol vertically to a new position in the outline. The heading moves along with any subheadings and subtext.

TO SELECT A LEVEL OF HEADINGS TO VIEW IN THE OUTLINE

Click a button from 1 to 9 (or All) in the Outline bar. To expand or collapse the subheadings or subtext under a selected heading, click the Expand or Collapse button—the sixth and seventh buttons on the Outline bar.

TO SELECT A NUMBERING FORMAT FOR AN OUTLINE

1. Select the entire outline. (Hold down the Ctrl key and click the mouse in the selection bar.)
2. Choose Tools ➤ Bullets and Numbering. Select the Outline option button at the top of the Bullets and Numbering dialog box.
3. Choose one of the available numbering formats in the Format list.
4. Optionally, click the Auto Update check box. This option inserts fields into your outline for the numbering system and updates the numbers if you reorganize your outline.
5. Click OK.

Shortcut: Select the outline and click the Numbered List button in the Toolbar.

SEE ALSO

Normal View, Numbered Lists, Page Layout View, Styles

PAGE BREAKS

As you enter pages of text, Word automatically creates *soft page breaks* at appropriate positions in a document. If you later insert or delete text, Word repaginates the document accordingly. You can enter a *hard page break* at any position where you want text to begin at the top of a new page. When Word repaginates the document, any hard breaks you have created remain unchanged.

TO CREATE A HARD PAGE BREAK

Move the insertion point to the position where you want the page to break. Then choose Insert ➤ Break and click OK to accept the default Page Break option.

Shortcut: Position the insertion point and press Ctrl-↵.

NOTE

In Normal view a soft page break appears as a light dotted line across the page and a hard page break appears as a dark dotted line. In Page Layout view you can see the actual page outlines for each page break.

SEE ALSO

Formatting Pages, Normal View, Page Layout View, Widows and Orphans

PAGE LAYOUT VIEW

In Page Layout view you can see all the elements of your document as they will appear on the printed page—including text, graphics, columns, frames, headers, footers, footnotes, and so on.

TO SWITCH TO PAGE LAYOUT VIEW

Choose View ➤ Page Layout.

NOTE

Word repaginates your document when you switch to Page Layout view.

SEE ALSO

Draft Mode, Outlining, Normal View, Zooming

PAGE NUMBERS

To create a header or a footer that displays only the page number, you can use the Page Numbers command.

TO INSERT PAGE NUMBERS

1. Choose Insert ➤ Page Numbers. The Page Numbers dialog box displays options for the position and alignment of the page numbers.

2. Click the Top of Page (Header) or Bottom of Page (Footer) option in the Position box.

3. Click Left, Center, or Right in the Alignment box.

4. Optionally, click the Format button to choose a format for the page numbers. In the Page Number Format dialog box, pull down the Number Format list and select Arabic numerals (the default), lowercase or uppercase letters, or lowercase or uppercase Roman numerals. Then click OK on both dialog boxes.

NOTES

When you use the Page Numbers command to insert page numbers, Word automatically activates the Different First Page option in the Header/Footer dialog box. As a result, the page number does not display on the first page of your document. To display the first page number, choose View ➤ Header/Footer, and remove the X from the Different First Page option.

To insert a page number along with other text in a header or a footer, choose View ➤ Normal and then View ➤ Header/Footer to open a header or footer pane and click the Page Number button. Both the Insert ➤ Page Number command and the Page Number button insert a PAGE field into the header or footer; Word updates this field to create the correct page numbers throughout your document.

SEE ALSO

Fields, Headers and Footers, Indexing, Page Layout View, Table of Contents

PAGE ORIENTATIONS

Word's Page Setup command offers two orientations for text on the printed page: portrait and landscape. On standard 8½×11″ paper, the Portrait option prints lines of text across the 8½″ width, and the Landscape option prints lines across the 11″ length of the paper.

TO CHANGE THE PAGE ORIENTATION

Choose Format ➤ Page Setup and click the Size and Orientation option button. Then click Portrait or Landscape in the Orientation box. The Sample box illustrates the appearance of the printed page.

NOTE

Word applies the Top, Bottom, Right, and Left margin settings (in the Page Setup dialog box) in relation to the way you read the text. For example, Top always specifies the margin above the first line of text and Bottom the margin below the last line, regardless of the page orientation.

SEE ALSO

Formatting Pages, Margins, Printing

PANES

For two concurrent views of the same document, you can split a window into two *panes*, one on top of the other. Each pane has its own vertical scroll bar, allowing you to examine two distant passages of the document at once.

TO SPLIT A DOCUMENT WINDOW INTO PANES

Double-click the *split bar,* the small, black rectangle located at the top of the vertical scroll bar. This divides the window into two panes of equal size. (Alternatively, you can drag the split bar down to any position along the scroll bar. When you point to the split bar, the mouse pointer takes the shape of two horizontal lines with two arrows pointing up and down.)

SEE ALSO

Window Arrangements

POINT SIZE

Each available type font supports a range of point sizes. You can use the Character command or the ribbon to change the point size in a selection of text.

TO CHANGE THE POINT SIZE

Select the text you want to change and choose Format ➤ Character. In the Character dialog box select a new size from the Points list.

Shortcut: Enter a new value into the Points box on the ribbon. Word accepts entries from 4 to 127 in this box. One inch is equivalent to 72 points.

SEE ALSO

Fonts, Formatting Text, Spacing between Characters

PREVIEWING

The Print Preview command displays a special preview window in which you can see how your document will look on the printed page. You can view one or two pages at a time and you can use tools in the preview window to make visual adjustments in margins, header and footer positions, and page break locations.

TO VIEW A DOCUMENT IN THE PRINT PREVIEW WINDOW

Choose File ➤ Print Preview. Click the One Page or Two Pages button to change the number of pages displayed in the preview window. To scroll through the pages of your document, use the vertical scroll bar at the right side of the window or press the PgUp or PgDn keys.

TO ADJUST MARGINS, HEADERS, FOOTERS, AND HARD PAGE BREAKS

Click the Margins button in the preview window. Word marks each of the four margins as a line with a handle. Drag a handle to change the position of a margin. (As you do so, the margin's numeric setting is displayed at the upper-right corner of the preview window.) You can also drag the document's header or footer slightly up or down within the top or bottom margin area. Finally, you can drag soft or hard page-break lines to new positions in the document. To see how these adjustments change your document, click the Margin button again.

NOTE

You can print the document from the preview window by clicking the Print button. In response, Word displays the Print dialog box.

SEE ALSO

Headers and Footers, Margins, Page Breaks, Printing

PRINT MERGE

To print personalized copies of a form letter or other document, you perform the steps of the print-merge operation. A print merge requires two documents—a *main document* and a *data file*. The main document contains the basic text of the form document, along with *merge field names* that mark places where specific items of information will be inserted for each copy of the letter. The data file supplies individual records of information that Word merges into the main document for each printed copy.

TO PRINT PERSONALIZED COPIES OF A FORM DOCUMENT

1. Open a new document window for creating a data file. Use the Insert Table command or the Table button to insert a blank table with the appropriate dimensions for the data. (See *Tables* for detailed information about creating tables.) Enter one-word field names for the data file in the first row of the table. In each subsequent row, enter one record of information. Save the data file to disk and close it.

2. Type the text of the main document. Optionally, insert a marker of your own choosing (such as XX) at each position where you want to insert variable information. Save your document to disk, but leave it open.

3. Choose File ➤ Print Merge. A pictorial dialog box named Print Merge Setup appears on the screen.

4. Click the Attach Data File button. In the resulting dialog box, select or enter the name of your data file in the File Name text box, then click OK. The data file is now attached to your main document, and the print-merge bar appears above the document. (At the right side of the print-merge bar, you can see the name of the attached data file.)

5. Move the insertion point to the position where you want to insert the first item of variable information into the document. (If you have entered temporary markers such as XX into your document, you can use the Edit ➤ Find command to find and select each marker in turn.)

6. Click the Insert Merge Field button in the print merge-bar. In the resulting Insert Merge Field dialog box, you'll find a list of the field names from the attached data file. Select the field name that represents the variable information you want to insert at the current position and click OK. Word inserts a merge field name into your document, and encloses the name within angle brackets. (The merge field names replace any temporary markers you've included in your documents.)

7. Repeat steps 5 and 6 for each merge field name that you want to insert into the main document. After inserting all the merge field names, click the Save button to save the main document to disk.

8. Click the Merge to Printer button, the last button in the print-merge bar. Word prints one copy of the main document for each record in your data file, replacing the merge field names with the items of information from the record.

EXAMPLE

See the following figures in Lesson 8 for illustrations of print merge: Figure 8.1 shows a main print merge document before the insertion of merge field names, and Figure 8.2 shows a data file with the row of field names at the top of the table. In Figure 8.3 you can see the Print Merge Setup dialog box. Figures 8.4 and 8.5 show the print-merge bar and the Insert Merge Field dialog box. Finally, Figure 8.6 displays the main document with the merge field names inserted at appropriate locations, and Figure 8.7 gives an example of a final printed copy of the form letter.

NOTES

You can save the row of field names for a data file in a separate *header file*. (You might want to do this if a given set of field names applies to more than one data file.) Choose File ➤ Print Merge and click the Attach Header File button to attach the header file to the main document. Then choose the Print Merge command again and click Attach Data File to attach the data file. Both file names will be displayed at the right side of the print-merge bar.

If you want guidance in creating a data file, click the Create Data File button in the Attach Data File dialog box. Word displays a series of dialog boxes and other tools that will help you create the data table and fill it in with data. However, if you already have experience with creating and working with tables in Word, you will probably prefer to create the data file on your own.

A merge field name is actually a MERGEFIELD field. If you want to view or edit a MERGEFIELD, press Shift-F9 to view the field codes.

SEE ALSO

Fields, Mailing Labels, Tables

PRINTING

The Print command gives you options for printing all or part of a document or any other information that is saved along with the document.

TO PRINT ALL OR PART OF A DOCUMENT

1. Open or activate the document that you want to print. If you want to print only one selected page, move the insertion point to the page.

2. Choose File ➤ Print. In the Print dialog box, make sure the Document option is selected in the Print list.

3. Adjust the setting in the Copies text box if you want to print more than one copy of your document. (An X in the Collate Copies check box means that Word will print all the pages of one copy before beginning the next copy. If you want to print uncollated copies, click the check box to remove the X.)

4. In the Range box, select All to print the entire document, Current Page to print the page where the insertion point is located, or Pages to print a specific range of pages. For the Pages option, enter page numbers into the From and To boxes.

5. Click OK.

Shortcut: Click the Print button in the Toolbar to print the entire document.

NOTES

To print a block of text from your document, select the text and then choose File ➤ Print. Click the Selection option in the Range box and click OK.

If you need to select or set up a Windows printer, click the Setup button in the Print dialog box. Select the printer in the Print Setup dialog box and click Setup to view the current options for your printer. (Alternatively, choose File ➤ Print Setup.)

You can direct the printed output to a file on disk instead of the printer. To do so, check the Print to File option in the Print dialog box. Word prompts you to enter a name for the print file. This operation does not change your document file.

To print more than one file in a single operation, choose File ➤ Find File. In the File Name list, select the files you want to print. (To select multiple files in the list, hold down the Ctrl key and click each file name.) Then click the Print button.

TO PRINT OTHER INFORMATION

Choose File ➤ Print and select an option from the Print list:

◆ Summary Info prints entries from the Summary Info box.

◆ Annotations prints any annotations contained in the document.

◆ Styles prints styles used in the current document.

◆ Glossary prints global and template glossary entries.

◆ Key Assignments prints information about macros.

NOTE

To print special categories of information along with your document, click the Options button in the Print dialog box. In the Include with Document box, check any combination of options: Summary Info, Field Codes, Annotations, Hidden Text.

SEE ALSO

Finding a File, Formatting Pages, Page Orientations, Print Merge, Printing Envelopes, Summary Information, Widows and Orphans

PRINTING ENVELOPES

The Create Envelope command prints addresses on an envelope.

TO PRINT AN ENVELOPE

1. Optionally, open or activate a letter that contains the address you want to print. Select the lines of the address.

2. Choose Tools ➤ Create Envelope to open the Create Envelope dialog box. (If you have selected an address in the current document, it appears in the Addressed To box. If you have recorded a mailing address in the User Info category of the Options command, it appears in the Return Address box.)

3. If necessary, revise or enter the addresses in the Addressed To and Return Address boxes. Check the Omit Return Address option if you do not want to print the entry that appears in the Return Address box.

4. Pull down the Envelope Size list and choose one of the standard envelope formats from the list.

5. Make sure you have placed an envelope in your printer. Click the Print Envelope button.

Shortcut: Click the Envelope button in the Toolbar to open the Create Envelope dialog box.

NOTES

To use an envelope feeder with the Create Envelope command, choose Tools ➤ Options, click the Print category, and check the option labeled Printer's Envelope Feeder has been Installed.

To record your return address, choose Tools ➤ Options. Click the User Info icon in the Category list, and type an entry in the Mailing Address box. (Press Shift-⏎ to enter a new line of text in this box.)

SEE ALSO

Mailing Labels

QUOTATION MARKS

Word provides special codes for entering curled quotation marks into a document. You type these codes on the numeric keypad.

TO ENTER A CURLED QUOTATION MARK

1. If necessary, press the Num Lock key to activate the numeric keypad. (*NUM* appears in the status bar.)

2. Hold down the Alt key and type a four-digit code at the numeric keypad:

   - Alt-0145 for a single opening-quotation mark.
   - Alt-0146 for a single closing-quotation mark.
   - Alt-0147 for a double opening-quotation mark.
   - Alt-0148 for a double closing-quotation mark.

3. Optionally, press Num Lock again to deactivate the keypad. (NUM disappears from the status bar.)

EXAMPLE

In the following text you can compare the appearance of straight and curled quotation marks:

When asked his reaction to the recent press reports he replied, "I have nothing to say about that at this time."

When asked his reaction to the recent press reports he replied, "I have nothing to say about that at this time."

NOTE

If you prefer to use curled quotation marks, you'll probably want to create macros to enter them into a document.

SEE ALSO

Dashes, Macros, Symbols

REPLACING TEXT AND STYLES

Using the Replace command, you can perform search-and-replace operations on specific text entries or formatting patterns in a document.

TO REPLACE TEXT

1. Choose Edit ➤ Replace to open the Replace dialog box. Enter the text that you want to replace in the Find What text box.

2. Enter the replacement text in the Replace With text box.

3. Place an X in the Match Whole Word Only check box if you want to replace only whole word occurrences rather than letters embedded within a word. Place an X in the Match Case check box if you want Word to search for text in the exact uppercase/lowercase pattern you have entered into the Find What box.

4. Click the Find Next button to search for the text. If the text is found, Word scrolls to its location in your document and selects it. Click the Replace button to replace the selection. Repeat this step for each occurrence you want to replace.

5. Click the Close button to close the Replace dialog box.

Shortcut: If you want to replace all the occurrences of the Find What entry, click the Replace All button to make all the replacements at once, then click the Close button. (If you change your mind after the replace operation is complete, click the Undo button before doing anything else.)

NOTE

In the Find What text box you can use the question mark (?) to represent an unspecified character. For example, *t??e* matches any four-letter word that begins with *t* and ends with *e*. In both the Find What and Replace With boxes you can use the caret symbol (^) along with a letter to represent certain special characters; for example, *^t* represents a tab character and *^p* a paragraph mark.

TO REPLACE FORMATTING PATTERNS OR FORMATTED TEXT

1. Choose Edit ➤ Replace.2.

If you want to search for a format pattern without text, delete the contents of the Find What text box (or leave the box empty). On the other hand, if you want to search for a combination of text and formatting, enter the text into the Find What box.

2. Click one or all of the Character, Paragraph, or Styles buttons, in any order. In the resulting dialog boxes, select the formatting patterns that you want to search for. A description of the formatting search pattern appears just beneath the Find What text box.

3. Optionally, place an X in the Match Whole Word Only or the Match Case check box.

4. Activate the Replace With text box. Specify the formatting patterns that you want to apply to the replacements.

5. Click the Find Next button to find the first occurrence. Then click the Replace button if you want to replace the selection. Repeat this step for each replacement, or click Replace All to perform all the replacements at once.

Shortcut: In the Find What and Replace With text boxes, you can use familiar keyboard shortcuts to specify formatting (instead of clicking the Character or Paragraph buttons). For example, press Ctrl-B, Ctrl-I, or Ctrl-U for bold, italics or underlining replacements; and Ctrl-L, Ctrl-E, Ctrl-R, and Ctrl-J for left-alignment, centering, right-alignment, or justification.

EXAMPLE

Here is how to replace all occurrences of a particular sequence of italic text with the same text in bold: Choose Edit ➤ Replace. Enter the text into the Find What text box and press Ctrl-I to search for italic formatting. Then activate the Replace With box. Enter the same text and click Ctrl-B to replace with bold formatting. Click the Replace All button to make the replacements.

NOTE

To clear formatting patterns, activate the Find What or Replace With box and click the Clear button.

SEE ALSO

Finding Text and Styles, Formatting Paragraphs, Formatting Text, Styles

REVISION MARKS

The Revision Marks command gives you a visual way to keep track of the revisions made in a document. You can also use the command to accept or reject revisions.

TO MARK THE REVISIONS IN A DOCUMENT

1. Choose Tools ➤ Revision Marks.

2. In the Revision Marks dialog box, place an X in the Mark Revisions check box.

3. Optionally, make a new selection in the Revision Bars box. (Word displays vertical revision bars to highlight all lines that contain revisions.)

4. Optionally, make a new selection in the Mark New Text With box. This selection determines how Word will display insertions in the document.

5. Click OK, then begin revising the document. Word displays revision marks for deletions, insertions, replacements, and moves, as shown here:

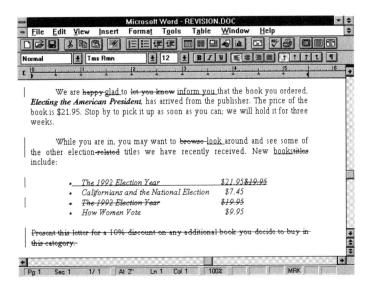

TO ACCEPT OR REJECT
REVISIONS IN A DOCUMENT

Move the insertion point to the top of the revised document, and choose Tools ➤ Revision Marks. To accept all the revisions at once, click the Accept Revisions button. To reject all the revisions at once, click the Undo Revisions button. (In each case, Word displays a dialog box asking for confirmation. Click Yes.) Alternatively, to search for revisions and judge them one at a time, click the Search button repeatedly and click either Accept Revisions or Undo Revisions for each change.

TO COMPARE TWO
FILE VERSIONS OF A DOCUMENT

Open the original document and then choose Tools ➤ Compare Versions. In the Compare Versions dialog box, select the revised file in the File Name list. Then click OK. In response, Word places revision marks in the original document to represent the differences between the two versions.

SEE ALSO

Deleting Text, Moving Text

RIBBON

The ribbon is an option bar displayed just beneath the Toolbar. It displays a Style box, a Font box, a Points box, three text formatting buttons (Bold, Italics, and Underline), four alignment buttons (Left Align, Center, Right Align, and Justify), four tab buttons, and the Show/Hide ¶ button.

TO DISPLAY OR HIDE THE RIBBON

Choose View ➤ Ribbon.

SEE ALSO

Aligning, Formatting Text, Fonts, Points, Styles, Tabs, Special Characters

RULER

The ruler is the option bar displayed at the top of each document window. It can display any one of three different scales: paragraph, margin, and table. On the paragraph scale you can adjust the indents for one or more paragraphs of text. On the margin scale you can drag the left and right margins. On the table scale (displayed when the insertion point is in a table) you can change column widths in a table.

TO DISPLAY A DIFFERENT SCALE ON THE RULER

Click the symbol displayed at the left side of the ruler.

TO DISPLAY OR HIDE THE RULER

Choose View ➤ Ruler.

SEE ALSO

Hanging Indents, Indenting, Margins, Tables

SAVING

Word provides simple techniques for naming and saving a new document and for saving your work in an existing file.

TO SAVE A NEW DOCUMENT FOR THE FIRST TIME

Choose File ➤ Save As. Use the Directories and Drives boxes to specify the path location for saving the file. Enter a name for the new file in the File Name box, then click OK.

Shortcut: Click the Save button in the Toolbar to open the Save As dialog box.

NOTE

You can also use the Save As command to save a second copy of the current document under a different name.

TO SAVE YOUR WORK IN AN EXISTING FILE

Choose File ➤ Save or click the Save button.

TO SAVE ALL OPEN DOCUMENTS

Choose File ➤ Save All. Word asks you to confirm each save operation.

NOTE

The Save All command also saves any newly created templates, glossary entries, and macros.

TO ACTIVATE THE AUTOMATIC SAVE FEATURE

1. Choose Tools ➤ Options and click the Save icon in the Categories list.
2. Place an X in the Automatic Save Every check box.
3. Optionally, adjust the setting in the Minutes box. By default, Word saves your files every 10 minutes when you activate this option.

SEE ALSO

Backups, Converting Document Formats, Deleting a Document from Disk, Opening a File, Options for Word Settings

SECTIONS

To apply distinct formats to different portions of a document, you can divide the document into sections. For example, a section division allows you to display one selection of text in newspaper-style columns without changing the format of the rest of the document. You can use the Section Layout command to select a vertical orientation for a section, and to display line numbers within the section.

TO INSERT A SECTION BREAK

1. Move the insertion point to where you want to insert the break.
2. Choose Insert ➤ Break.
3. Click an option in the Section Break box: The Next Page option starts the section on a new page. The Continuous option inserts a section break without creating a page break. The Even Page and Odd Page options start the break at a specified numbered page.
4. Click OK. In Normal view the section break is marked by a double dotted line. In Page Layout view, there is no visible section marker, but the status line always identifies the section number where the insertion point is.

EXAMPLE

See *Lesson 5* for several examples of section formatting. In the newsletter shown in Figures 5.1 and 5.2, there is a section break between the one-column banner on page 1 and the two-column text beneath the banner.

NOTE

You can define distinct headers and footers for each section in a document.

TO CHANGE THE VERTICAL ALIGNMENT OF THE TEXT IN A SECTION

Move the insertion point into the section, select Format ➤ Section Layout, and select an option from the Vertical Alignment box:

- Top aligns the text beneath the top margin.
- Center centers the text between the top and bottom margins.
- Justify inserts extra space between paragraphs so that the text meets both the top and bottom margins.

TO DISPLAY LINE NUMBERS IN A SECTION

1. Move the insertion point into the section, and choose Format ➤ Section Layout.
2. Click the Line Numbers button in the Section Layout dialog box.
3. In the Line Numbers dialog box, place an X in the Add Line Numbering check box. Optionally, adjust the Start at #, From Text, and Count By settings. Then click the OK buttons on the Line Numbers and Section Layout dialog boxes.

NOTE

To view the line numbering, choose File ➤ Print Preview.

TO DELETE A SECTION BREAK

In Normal view, position the insertion point just after the section break and press the Backspace key.

NOTE

The formatting for a section is attached to the section break; when you delete the break, you also delete the section formatting.

SEE ALSO

Columns, Headers and Footers

SELECTING TEXT

Using the mouse, the keyboard, and the *selection bar* (the unmarked column at the left side of the text in a document), you can quickly select any portion of text. You can also select *columns* of text, using the right mouse button.

TO SELECT TEXT

- ◆ A *word:* Double click the mouse over the word.
- ◆ A *line:* Click the mouse in the selection bar next to the line.
- ◆ A *sentence:* Hold down the Ctrl key and click the sentence with the mouse.
- ◆ A *paragraph:* Double-click in the selection bar next to the paragraph.
- ◆ *The entire document:* Hold down the Ctrl key and click the mouse anywhere in the selection bar.

TO SELECT TEXT USING THE KEYBOARD ALONE

Hold down the Shift key and press any combination of arrow and direction keys (↑ ↓ ← → Home, End, PgUp, PgDn) to make the selection.

TO SELECT A COLUMN OF TEXT

Position the mouse pointer at a corner of the column. Then hold down the *right* mouse button and drag the mouse through the area of the column.

SEE ALSO

Outlining, Tables

SHADING

Using the Border command, you can apply gray shading or colored backgrounds to a selection of text.

TO APPLY SHADING TO A SELECTION

1. Move the insertion point into the line, paragraph, or frame that you want to shade.

2. Choose Format ➤ Border. In the Border Paragraphs dialog box, choose a border style if you want to display a border around the shading.

3. Click the Shading button. The Shading dialog box contains lists of colors in the Foreground and Background boxes and a list of patterns in the Pattern box.

4. Select a color or a gray shade from the Background list. Optionally, make selections from the Foreground and Pattern lists as well. Click the OK buttons on the Shading and Border Paragraph dialog boxes.

EXAMPLE

The first letter in the following paragraph is framed, bordered, and shaded:

You can use the Frame button and the Border command to create a *dropped capital letter* in a border with shading. Select the first letter in a paragraph and increase its point size. Then click the Frame button to insert a frame around the letter. Choose the Border command from the Format menu and apply a border and shading to the frame. If necessary, choose the Frame command from the Format menu to adjust the space between the frame and its surrounding text.

SEE ALSO

Borders, Frames

SORTING

The Sorting command rearranges lists or tables of data in alphabetic, numeric, or chronological order.

TO SORT A LIST OF NAMES, NUMBERS, OR DATES

1. Select a list in which each entry is on a separate line.

2. Choose Tools ➤ Sorting.

3. In the Sorting dialog box click the Ascending or Descending option. (Ascending means alphabetical order for text and chronological order for dates.)

4. In the Key Type list choose the type of data in the list: Alphanumeric, Numeric, or Date. (Optionally, place an X in the Case Sensitive check box for a case-sensitive, alphanumeric sort.) Make sure the Field Number setting is 1. Then click OK.

NOTE

The Sorting command recognizes dates in a variety of formats, including *9/17/92* and *Sept 17, 1992*.

TO SORT COLUMNS OF DATA

1. Enter the columns of data separated by tabs or commas or choose Table ➤ Insert Table to create a table of data.

2. Select the rows and columns of data you want to sort and choose Tools ➤ Sorting.

3. Change the Field Number setting to identify the column by which you want to sort the data. (For example, enter 2 to sort by the second column or 3 to sort by the third.)

4. Click Ascending or Descending for the sorting order and choose an option from the Key Type list to indicate the type of data in the selected column (Alphanumeric, Numeric, or Date).

5. Click Comma or Tab to identify the separator between columns. (These option buttons are dimmed if the data is arranged in a table.)

6. Click OK.

EXAMPLE

The following employee information is arranged in columns separated by tabs; initially the table is in alphabetical order by employee names:

EMPLOYEE	SALARY	DATE HIRED
Andrews, M.	$52,350	Sept 18, 1990
Marshall, J.	$28,200	Feb 15, 1988
Smith, L.	$44,950	Dec 15, 1991
Wilson, T.	$35,400	May 5, 1990

To sort the table in ascending order by salaries, select the four rows of employees (not including the top row of column headings) and choose Tools ➤ Sorting. Click Ascending and select the Numeric option in the Key Type list. Click the Tab option button. Enter **2** into the Field Number list. Here is the result:

EMPLOYEE	SALARY	DATE HIRED
Marshall, J.	$28,200	Feb 15, 1988
Wilson, T.	$35,400	May 5, 1990
Smith, L.	$44,950	Dec 15, 1991
Andrews, M.	$52,350	Sept 18, 1990

To arrange the employees by length of employment—starting from the most recently hired—click Descending, choose the Date option, and enter **3** for the Field Number:

EMPLOYEE	SALARY	DATE HIRED
Smith, L.	$44,950	Dec 15, 1991
Andrews, M.	$52,350	Sept 18, 1990
Wilson, T.	$35,400	May 5, 1990
Marshall, J.	$28,200	Feb 15, 1988

NOTE

To restore the previous order of a list or table, click the Undo button immediately after the sort.

S

SEE ALSO

Selecting Text, Tables, Tabs

SPACING BETWEEN CHARACTERS

You can use the Character command to increase or decrease the amount of space between characters in a selection of text.

TO CONDENSE OR EXPAND A SELECTION OF TEXT

1. Select the text and choose Format ➤ Character.

2. In the Spacing list, choose the Expanded or Condensed option. (The default option is Normal.)

3. Optionally, adjust the point measurement in the By box. You can condense the text by as much as 1.75 points or expand it by as much as 14 points.

4. Click OK.

EXAMPLES

Here are examples of normal, condensed, and expanded text:

This is an example of normal spacing.	This text is condensed by 1 point.	This text is expanded by 3 points.

NOTE

Changing the amount of space between letters is called *kerning*.

SEE ALSO

Formatting Text

SPACING BETWEEN LINES

You can use the Paragraph command to increase or decrease the amount of space between lines in a paragraph and the amount of space before and after a paragraph.

TO CHANGE THE SPACE BETWEEN LINES

1. Move the insertion point into the paragraph that you want to change and choose Format ➤ Paragraph.
2. Select an option from the Line Spacing list or adjust the At setting. The resulting line spacing is depicted in the Sample box.
3. Optionally, change the spacing measurements in the Before and After boxes.
4. Click OK.

Shortcut: Press Ctrl-1, Ctrl-2, or Ctrl-5 for single spacing, double spacing, or 1½ spacing.

NOTE

Word automatically adjusts the line spacing when you increase the point size of one or more characters in a line.

SEE ALSO

Formatting Paragraphs

SPECIAL CHARACTERS

Word represents the nonprinting elements of a document—including spaces, tabs, paragraph divisions, optional hyphens, and hidden text—with special marks and characters that are normally hidden from view. You may want to view these characters occasionally to see exactly how a document is organized.

TO VIEW SPECIAL CHARACTERS

Choose Tools ➤ Options and click the View icon in the Categories list. In the Nonprinting Characters box, place an X in the check box for characters that you want to view or check the All box to view all special characters.

Shortcut: Click the Show/Hide ¶ button on the ribbon to view or hide the special characters in a document.

EXAMPLE

Examine Figure 2.3 in *Lesson 2* for a display of special characters in a document.

SEE ALSO

Hiding Text, *Hyphenation*, *Tabs*

SPELLING CHECKS

The Spelling command reviews all or part of your document for possible spelling errors.

TO CHECK THE SPELLING OF A DOCUMENT

1. Select the word, sentence, or paragraphs you want to check or move the insertion point to the beginning of the document to check all the text.

2. Choose Tools ➤ Spelling. Word begins checking your document and opens the Spelling dialog box if any errors are found. Each potential spelling error appears in the Not in Dictionary box, and a suggested correction appears in the Change To box. Other suggestions are listed in the Suggestions box. Click the Change button to replace the misspelled word in the document or click Ignore to reject the suggestion. (Click Change All or Ignore all to treat the word identically throughout the document.) Alternatively, click the Add button to insert the current word into the dictionary for use in future spelling checks.

Shortcut: Select a word or other portion of text and click the Spelling button in the Toolbar.

EXAMPLE

Examine Figures 4.4 and 4.5 in *Lesson 4* for examples of the Spelling dialog boxes.

NOTE

To change the operation of the Spelling command, choose Tools ➤ Options and click the Spelling icon in the Category list or click the Options button in the Spelling dialog box.

Choose the Format ➤ Language command to mark words in foreign languages or to instruct Word to skip certain selections of your document during a spelling check.

SEE ALSO

Grammar Checks, Languages, Thesaurus

SPIKE

The *Spike* is a special glossary entry that you can use to perform cumulative cut-and-paste operations.

TO INSERT A SELECTION INTO THE SPIKE

Select any combination of text and graphics and press Ctrl-F3. The selection is removed from your document and appended to the end of the Spike.

NOTE

You can add to the contents of the Spike by making another selection and pressing Ctrl-F3 again. Word appends each new selection to the end of the spike.

TO MOVE THE CONTENTS OF THE SPIKE INTO A DOCUMENT

Move the insertion point to where you want to paste the contents and press Ctrl-Shift-F3. The entire contents of the Spike appear at the current position in your document. After this operation the Spike is empty.

TO COPY THE CONTENTS OF THE SPIKE

Type the glossary name **spike** at the location where you want to copy the contents and press F3. The contents of the Spike are copied to your document and take the place of the glossary name. This operation does *not* empty the Spike; its contents remain unchanged.

NOTE

The Spike does not use the Clipboard. The contents of the Clipboard are un-affected by your use of the Spike.

SEE ALSO

Copying Text, Glossary Entries, Moving Text, Selecting Text

STATUS BAR

The status bar—located at the bottom of the Word window—supplies messages, prompts, and information about the current document. The location of the inser-tion point is described in several ways: the page number, the section, the distance from the top of the page, the line number, and column number. At the right side of the status bar Word displays the status of keyboard toggles and other switches.

TO HIDE THE STATUS BAR

Choose Tools ➤ Options and click the View icon in the Category list. In the Win-dow box, remove the X from the Status Bar check box.

NOTE

Double-click the status bar to open the Go To dialog box.

SEE ALSO

Go To, Options for Word Settings, Ribbon, Ruler, Sections

STYLES

A style is a combination of formatting options identified by a name in the ribbon's style list. Word defines several *standard styles* for specific uses—such as headings, footers and headers, and footnotes. You can create your own styles by assigning names to formatting patterns that you use frequently. You can then save a style definition as a permanent part of a document or template.

TO CREATE A STYLE BY EXAMPLE

1. Apply a combination of formats to a selection of text. Then select the formatted text and choose Format ➤ Style. In the Style dialog box, a list of the current formats appears in the Description box.

2. Enter a name for this new style definition in the Style Name box. Optionally, enter a shortcut key for the style in the Key box. (You can later use this shortcut key to apply the style.)

3. Click the Define button to expand the Style dialog box. To save the new style in the current template, place an X in the Add to Template check box.

4. Click the Add button. Then click Close to close the Style dialog box.

Shortcut: Select some formatted text and enter a new style name directly into the style box in the ribbon.

NOTE

You can also define a style by selecting options from the Style dialog box. Choose Format ➤ Style and enter a name for the style. Click the Define button. Then click any combination of the Character, Paragraph, Tabs, Border, Frame, and Language buttons in turn and select formats from the resulting dialog boxes. (A list of the formats you have selected appears in the Description box.) Finally, click Add to define the style and click Close to close the Style dialog box. The new style name appears in the style list.

TO APPLY A STYLE TO A SELECTION

Select the text and choose the style name from the ribbon's style list.

Shortcut: If you have assigned a shortcut key to a style definition, you can press Ctrl-Shift-*key* to apply the style.

SEE ALSO

Formatting Paragraphs, Formatting Text, Ribbon, Templates

SUBSCRIPTS AND SUPERSCRIPTS

Using the Character command, you can display numbers or text in a subscript or superscript format, set slightly below or above the normal line of text.

TO FORMAT A SELECTION AS A SUBSCRIPT OR SUPERSCRIPT

1. Select the number or text that will become the subscript or superscript and choose Format ➤ Character.
2. In the Character dialog box, make a selection from the Super/Subscript list. The options are None (the default), Superscript, and Subscript.
3. Click OK.

Shortcuts: Press Ctrl-Shift-+ and then type the superscript text or press Ctrl-= and type the subscript text. To return to the normal line of text, press Ctrl-Shift-+ or Ctrl-= again.

NOTES

You can adjust the vertical displacement of a subscript or superscript by entering a point measurement in the By text box in the Character dialog box. To improve the visual effect, you may also want to display a subscript or superscript in a smaller point size than the rest of the text.

SEE ALSO

Equation Editor, Formatting Text, Point Size

SUMMARY INFORMATION

When you save a document for the first time, Word displays the Summary Info dialog box on the screen. In this box you can enter useful background information about your document: a title, a subject description, the name of the author (the installed user's name by default), a list of key words from the text of the document, and comments. Word saves this information along with the text of your document and you can review it at any time.

TO VIEW THE SUMMARY INFO BOX FOR AN OPEN DOCUMENT

Choose File ➤ Summary Info.

EXAMPLE

For an example of the Summary Info box, look at Figure 1.8 in *Lesson 1*.

NOTE

Click the Statistics button on the Summary Info box to view and update statistics that Word keeps about your document. The Document Statistics dialog box includes the dates and times the document was created and last saved; the number of times it has been saved to disk; the amount of editing time in minutes; and the number of pages, words, and characters in the document. This box also identifies the template on which the document is based.

TO VIEW THE SUMMARY INFO BOX FOR A UNOPENED DOCUMENT FILE

Choose File ➤ FileFind and select the name of the file in the File Name list. Then click the Summary button.

TO DISABLE WORD'S SUMMARY INFO PROMPT

Choose Tools ➤ Options and click the Save icon in the Category list. Remove the X from the Prompt for Summary Info check box, then click OK. Word subsequently omits the Summary Info prompt when you save a file for the first time.

SEE ALSO

Finding a File, Options for Word Settings, Printing, Saving

SYMBOLS

You can use the Symbols command to insert mathematical and technical operators, Greek letters, and other special symbols into a document.

TO INSERT A SYMBOL

Choose Insert ➤ Symbol. The Symbol dialog box appears on the screen:

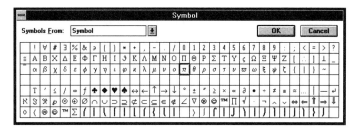

Select a character and click OK.

NOTE

You can pull down the Symbols From list to view a selection of other available symbol fonts.

SEE ALSO

Dashes, Equation Editor, Quotation Marks

TABLE OF CONTENTS

Word simplifies the process of creating a table of contents for a document. The easiest way to prepare for a table of contents is to apply Word's standard heading styles—*heading 1*, *heading 2*, and so on—to the headings of your document. (These are used automatically if you begin by planning your document in Outline mode.) When you choose the Table of Contents command, Word compiles the headings and inserts the page numbers.

TO CREATE A TABLE OF CONTENTS

1. Apply Word's standard heading styles to the headings in your document. Enter any amount of text beneath each heading.

2. Move the insertion point to the beginning of the document or to some other position where you want to insert the table of contents.

3. Choose Insert ➤ Table of Contents. In the resulting dialog box, keep the default option, Use Heading Paragraphs.

4. Optionally, enter the range of heading levels you want to include in the table of contents: Enter the beginning level in the From text box and the ending level in the To text box.

5. Click OK. Word inserts a TOC field at the insertion point. If you see the field codes rather than the table of contents itself, choose View ➤ Field Codes.

EXAMPLE

Here is an example of a table of contents, created from the employee handbook outline presented in *Lesson 9* (Figure 9.9):

Employee Handbook

NOTES

Because a table of contents is the result of a field, Word can update the pagination in the table if you change the length of text in the document itself. To update the page numbers, move the insertion point into the table of contents and press F9.

If you do not apply Word's standard heading styles to the headings in a document, you can use a different technique to create a table of contents. At the beginning of each part of your document, insert a TC field in the following format:

{TC "Heading Text" \L*x*}

The text in quotation marks can be any text that you want to appear as a heading in the table of contents. The \L instruction gives the heading level, where *x* is a number from 1 to 8. For example, this TC field identifies a second-level heading for the table of contents:

{TC "Chartres Cathedral" \L2}

(To insert a TC field, choose the Insert ➤ Field command and select the field name from the Field dialog box or press Ctrl-F9 and type the field codes directly into your document. Word formats TC fields as hidden text; to view them, click the Show/Hide ¶ button.)

After inserting these TC fields throughout the document, move the insertion point to the position where you want to build the table of contents and choose Insert ➤ Table of Contents. Choose the Use Table Entry Fields option and click OK.

SEE ALSO

Fields, Indexing, Outlining, Styles

TABLES

A table is an arrangement of rows and columns that you can insert into a document. The intersection of a row and a column is called a *cell*. A table is a versatile and convenient tool for displaying and formatting columns of numeric data or text.

TO INSERT A TABLE INTO A DOCUMENT

1. Move the insertion point to the position where you want to insert the table.

2. Choose Table ➤ Insert Table.

3. In the resulting dialog box, enter the number of columns and the number of rows you want in the table.

4. Optionally, enter a measurement for the width of columns in the table. Then click OK.

Shortcut: Click the Table button in the Toolbar. In the table grid that drops down beneath the button, drag the mouse pointer through the number of rows and columns you want in the new table. Then release the mouse button. Word creates the table at the insertion point.

EXAMPLES

Figure 7.3 in *Lesson 7* shows a table of numeric data. Figure 8.2 in *Lesson 8* shows a table organized as a data file for a print merge.

NOTES

Press the Tab key to move the insertion point from one cell to the next in a table. Inside a cell you can enter a number, a word, an entire block of text, a graphic, or any combination of these. Word-wrap takes place as you enter text into a cell, and each cell has its own selection bar along its left side. Word automatically increases the height of a row when you enter more than one line of text in a cell. To adjust the column width or the space between columns, choose Table ➤ ColumnWidth or drag the **T** markers along the table scale in the ruler.

By default, Word displays nonprinting gridlines to outline the rows and columns of a table. The Table ➤ Gridlines command is a toggle to turn this display on or off. If you want to *print* a border around a table or around each cell of a table, select the table and choose Format ➤ Border. The resulting dialog box gives you a choice between a border around the perimeter of the table or a grid outlining all the rows and columns of the table.

TO SELECT CELLS, ROWS, AND COLUMNS IN A TABLE

- *A cell:* Click in a cell's selection bar.
- *Multiple cells:* Drag the mouse through a series of adjacent cells.
- *A row:* Click just to the left of the row. Alternatively, double-click inside the selection bar of any cell in the row, or choose Table ➤ Select Row.
- *Consecutive rows:* Drag the mouse down the left side of the table alongside the rows you want to select.

- *A column:* Click just above the column. (The mouse pointer becomes a small black arrow.) Alternatively, click the right mouse button anywhere inside the column or choose Table ➤ Select Column.

- *Adjacent columns:* Drag the mouse just above the columns you want to select.

- *The entire table:* Move the insertion point into the table and choose Table ➤ Select Table. Alternatively, press Alt-5 (numeric keypad).

NOTE

After selecting cells, rows, or columns in a table, you can apply text and paragraph formatting to the selection.

TO INSERT OR DELETE COLUMNS

Select one or more columns in the table and choose Table ➤ Insert Columns or Table ➤ Delete Columns.

NOTE

To insert a column after the last column in the table, click just above and to the right of the table's upper-right corner cell, then choose Table ➤ Insert Column.

TO INSERT OR DELETE ROWS

Select one or more rows and choose Table ➤ Insert Rows or Table ➤ Delete Rows.

NOTE

To insert new rows after the bottom row in the table, move the insertion point to the line after the table and choose Table ➤ Insert Rows. In the Insert Rows dialog box, enter the number of rows you want to insert and click OK. To insert a single row after the bottom row, select the last cell in the table and press Tab.

TO CONVERT TABBED COLUMNS INTO A TABLE

Select the rows of tabbed data and click the Table button on the Toolbar. Word inserts a table with the appropriate number of rows and columns.

TO CONVERT A TABLE OF DATA INTO TEXT

Select the entire table and choose Table ➤ Convert Table to Text. In the resulting dialog box, choose a separator for the data: Paragraph Marks, Tabs, or Commas.

TO SPLIT A TABLE INTO TWO TABLES

Move the insertion point into the row where you want the split to be made, and choose Table ➤ Split Table. Word inserts a blank line at the split.

NOTE

To remove the split, delete the blank line; the two tables reunite.

SEE ALSO

Borders, Calculations, Graph, Mailing Labels, Print Merge, Ruler, Sorting

TABS

Using the Tabs command you can set tab stops for a new document or for an existing paragraph. You can also choose a *leader* to fill the width of a tab with characters. Word's default tab stops are marked at ½″ intervals on the ruler, but you can use the Tabs command to change this default.

TO SET TAB STOPS

1. Choose Format ➤ Tabs.
2. Enter a measurement in the Tab Stop Position box.
3. Click the Left, Center, Right, or Decimal option button in the Alignment box. This option determines how text will be aligned in relation to the tab stop.
4. Optionally, select a leader character in the Leader box. This option fills the width of a tab entry with periods, dashes, or underscore characters.
5. Click the Set button to set the tab.
6. Repeat steps 2 through 5 to set additional tab stops. Then click OK to close the Tab dialog box.

Shortcut: Select one of the four tab-alignment buttons in the ribbon, then click the mouse at the position on the ruler where you want to set the tab.

EXAMPLE

The following lines illustrate a left-aligned tab stop at the 1″ ruler position, and a decimal tab stop at the 3″ ruler position. The period has been selected as the leader character for the decimal tab:

Gross Income $35,971.88

Expenses . . . .(19,879.51)

Net Income $16,092.37

NOTE

When you set a tab stop at a position along the ruler, Word clears the default tab stops at the left of the new setting.

TO CLEAR TAB SETTINGS

Move the insertion point into the paragraph where you want to clear the tabs, then choose Format ➤ Tabs. To clear all the tab stops, click Clear All and then click OK. To clear tab stops individually, select an entry in the Tab Stop Position list and then click the Clear button. Repeat these steps for each tab that you want to clear, then click OK.

Shortcut: To clear a tab, use the mouse to drag the tab marker down from the ruler. When you release the mouse button, the tab is cleared.

NOTE

When you clear a tab setting, Word restores the default tab stops.

TO CHANGE THE INTERVAL FOR DEFAULT TABS

Choose Format ➤ Tab and enter a new measurement in the Default Tab Stops box. Then click OK. Word displays the new default tab stops along the ruler.

NOTE

You can view tab entries in a document by clicking the Show/Hide ¶ button on the ribbon. Each tab is represented by a right-arrow character.

SEE ALSO

Formatting Paragraphs, Ribbon, Ruler, Special Characters

TEMPLATES

A template is a collection of patterns and tools for creating a category of documents. You can create templates of your own, or you can use the general purpose templates that are included with Word. In a template you can store formats, text, graphics, headers, footers, glossary entries, macros, and styles. Every document is based on a template; the default is NORMAL.DOT.

TO CREATE A NEW TEMPLATE

1. Choose File ➤ New. In the New dialog box, click the Template option button.

2. Optionally, choose a template other than NORMAL.DOT on which to base the new template. (The new template takes on all the elements of the template it is based on.)

3. Click OK. Word opens a new template with a default name such as *Template1*, *Template2*, and so on.

4. Enter any text or graphics that you want to include as a standard part of the template. Optionally, define a header or a footer for the template.

5. Apply any combination of character, paragraph, and page formatting to the template. Then define any styles, macros, and glossary entries that you want to include in the template. When Word prompts you to specify where you want to store a new macro or glossary entry, click the *in Template* option.

6. Choose File ➤ Save As. Enter a name for the template and click OK.

NOTE

By default, Word adds a DOT extension to the template name and saves the file in the same directory as the Word program itself.

TO SELECT A TEMPLATE FOR A NEW DOCUMENT

Choose File ➤ New and select a template from the Use Template list. Then click OK. Word opens a new document based on the template you selected.

Shortcut: To open a new document based on NORMAL.DOT, click the New button, the first button in the Toolbar.

TO EDIT A TEMPLATE

Use the File ➤ Open command to open the template file. Then edit the contents of the template and choose File ➤ Save to save the revised version back to disk.

SEE ALSO

Formatting Pages, Formatting Paragraphs, Formatting Text, Glossary Entries, Headers and Footers, Macros, Styles

THESAURUS

The Thesaurus displays a list of synonyms for a selected word in a document. You can replace the original word with a synonym of your choice.

TO REPLACE A WORD WITH A SYNONYM

1. Move the insertion point next to the word you want to replace and choose Tools ➤ Thesaurus. The resulting Thesaurus dialog box displays a list of possible meanings for the selected word and a list of synonyms.

2. In the Meanings list, select the entry that most closely matches the context of the original word in your document. In response, the Synonyms box lists a group of synonyms for this meaning. (At the bottom of the Meanings list you may find two special entries called Related Words and Antonyms. Select one of these entries if you want to explore the sense of your word further.)

3. Select a word in the Synonyms box. Word copies your selection to the Replace With box. Click the Look Up button if you want to examine a new branch of synonyms. Optionally, repeat step 2.

4. When you find a suitable synonym, click the Replace button. Word closes the Thesaurus dialog box and replaces the selected word in your document with the synonym.

Shortcut: Move the insertion point next to the word you want to explore, and press Shift-F7 to open the Thesaurus dialog box.

EXAMPLE

Look at Figure 4.9 in *Lesson 4* for an example of the Thesaurus dialog box.

NOTES

Each time you click the Look Up button, the currently selected synonym is added to the Synonyms For list. If you want to return to a previous list of synonyms, pull down this list and select one of its entries.

To close the Thesaurus dialog box without replacing the selected word in your document, click the Cancel button.

Foreign-language Thesaurus tools are available from Microsoft.

SEE ALSO

Grammar Checks, Languages, Spelling Checks

TOOLBAR

The Toolbar is a line of buttons displayed just beneath the menu bar in the Word application window. The Toolbar buttons are shortcuts for commonly used menu commands. For example, you can click buttons to open or save a file; perform cut-and-paste and copy-and-paste procedures; undo the previous operation; create numbered and bulleted lists; insert tables, columns, frames, drawings, and graphs; print an envelope or a document; or check your spelling. You can customize the toolbar by defining buttons for macros you install in Word.

TO READ A DESCRIPTION OF A TOOLBAR BUTTON

Move the mouse pointer to the button in the Toolbar and hold down the left mouse button. A brief description appears in the status bar. (When you have read the description, move the mouse pointer back to the text area before releasing the mouse button.)

TO OPEN A HELP TOPIC
ABOUT A TOOLBAR BUTTON

Press Shift-F1 and then click the toolbar button with the mouse.

TO HIDE THE TOOLBAR FROM VIEW

Choose View ➤ Toolbar. (This command is a toggle. Choose it again to restore the Toolbar.)

NOTE

You can replace any button or space on the Toolbar with a button representing a macro. To view the options for customizing the Toolbar, choose Tools ➤ Options and click the Toolbar icon in the Category list. (See the *Macros* entry for details.)

SEE ALSO

Macros, Options for Word Settings, Ribbon, Ruler

UNDOING AN OPERATION

In many situations, you can choose the Undo command to reverse the effect of the previous operation you performed in Word.

TO UNDO AN OPERATION

Choose Edit ➤ Undo immediately after the operation you want to reverse. In the Edit menu, the Undo command identifies the operation that will be reversed—for example, Undo Typing, Undo Bullets, or Undo Paste.

Shortcuts: Click the Undo button in the Toolbar or press Ctrl-Z.

NOTES

After you choose Undo, the command is displayed as Undo Undo in the Edit menu. Choose this command to restore the effect of the previous operation.

When an operation cannot be reversed, Word displays Can't Undo at the top of the Edit menu.

WIDOWS AND ORPHANS

By default Word tries to avoid printing the first line of a paragraph alone at the end of a page (an *orphan*), or the last line of a paragraph at the top of a page (a *widow*). To accomplish this, Word may rearrange the *soft page breaks* in a document, leaving blank lines at the ends of some pages. You can use the Options command to change the way Word handles paragraphs that fall within page breaks.

TO CHANGE THE WIDOWS AND ORPHANS OPTION

Choose Tools ➤ Options and click the Print icon in the Category list. Click the Widow/Orphan Control check box to enable or disable this option. After you change the status of this option, Word repaginates the current document.

SEE ALSO

Page Breaks

WINDOW ARRANGEMENTS

So that you can easily perform operations between documents—such as copying or moving text—Word allows you to open as many as nine document windows at a time. You can even open two or more windows for viewing different parts of the same open file. The Arrange All command resizes all open document windows so that you can view them all at once on the screen.

TO ARRANGE THE OPEN DOCUMENTS ON THE SCREEN

Choose Window ➤ Arrange All. Word arranges all the open documents in the most convenient way possible.

EXAMPLE

Here is an arrangement of two open documents in the Word window:

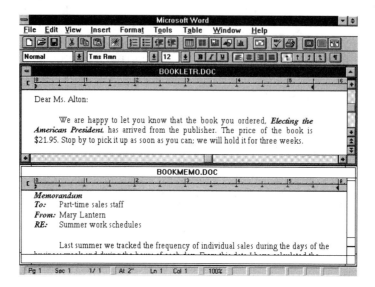

Notice that an individual ruler appears at the top of each document window.

NOTES

To activate an open document, click inside its window or press Ctrl-F6 repeatedly to cycle forward through the open windows. Press Ctrl-Shift-F6 to cycle backward through the windows.

To resize a document window individually, click the window's Restore button (if the Window is currently maximized) and drag any one of its four borders. To move a window, drag its title bar.

TO OPEN AN ADDITIONAL WINDOW FOR A DOCUMENT

Activate the target document and choose Window ➤ New Window. Word opens a second window for the document and appends the notation :2 after the file name in the second title bar.

NOTE

You can scroll each window independently. Changes you make in one window are also displayed in other windows for the same document.

SEE ALSO

Closing a Document, Copying Text, Opening a File, Links, Moving Text, Panes, Ruler

WORDART

In Microsoft WordArt you can create special typographical effects to incorporate into a Word document. The resulting graphic is inserted into your document as an *embedded object*.

TO CREATE A WORDART OBJECT

1. Move the insertion point to the location where you want to insert the WordArt object.
2. Choose Insert ➤ Object. The Object dialog box appears.
3. In the Object Type list box, choose the MS WordArt option and then click OK. The Microsoft WordArt application window appears.
4. Use the tools in WordArt to create textual effects: Type one or more lines of text into the box at the top of the application window and experiment with the options available in the Font, Size, Style, Fill, and Align lists.
5. When you have completed your WordArt object, click the OK button.

EXAMPLE

For an example of text effects created in Microsoft WordArt, see Figures 6.1, 6.2, and 6.3 in *Lesson 6*.

NOTE

Click the Help button to open the WordArt Help window. This window provides a general description of the program's features and capabilities.

TO CHANGE THE SIZE
AND SHAPE OF A WORDART OBJECT

1. Click the object to select it. Word displays eight sizing handles around the perimeter of the frame.

2. Drag any one of the sizing handles to increase or decrease the size.

TO WRAP TEXT
AROUND A WORDART OBJECT

Select the object and click the Frame button to insert a frame around it. Then drag the frame to any location in your document.

TO EDIT A WORDART OBJECT

Double-click the WordArt object in the document window. This restarts Microsoft WordArt and copies the object back into the application window.

SEE ALSO

Draw, Embedded Objects, Equation Editor, Frames, Graph

ZOOMING

Using the Zoom command you can enlarge your view of a page to as much as 200% of normal or you can reduce the view down to as little as 25% of normal. You can edit your document at any zoom setting.

TO ENLARGE OR REDUCE THE VIEW

Choose View ➤ Zoom and select an option from the Magnification box: 200%, 100%, 75%, or 50%. Alternatively, enter a zoom percentage (from 25 to 200) in the Custom box or click one of the two buttons at the bottom of the dialog box:

- The Page Width button reduces the view just enough to display the entire width of the page as it is currently formatted.

- The Whole Page button reduces the view enough to display the entire width and height of the page within the available work area in the Word window. (The dimensions of the work area may vary depending on whether you display the option bars.) This view appears to be similar to the Print Preview window; but in the Whole Page view you can actually continue to edit your document.

Shortcut: Click one of the three buttons at the far-right side of the Toolbar:

- The Zoom Whole Page button is equivalent to the Whole Page button in the Zoom dialog box.

- The Zoom 100 Percent button returns the zoom setting to 100% and switches into Normal view.

- The Zoom Page Width button is equivalent to the Page Width button in the Zoom bar.

NOTE

The status bar shows the current zoom percentage.

SEE ALSO

Formatting Pages, Normal View, Page Layout View, Previewing

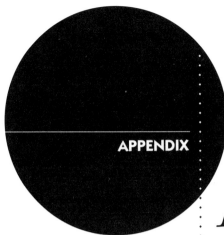

INSTALLING WORD FOR WINDOWS

Word installation takes about a half an hour. Before you start, check to see how much space is available on your hard disk. The full program—with all its features and components—requires 15 Mb. If less than that is available, do your best to free up the necessary space: Copy old data files to floppy disks and erase them from your hard disk. Delete any other files or directories that you are *sure* you don't need any more. (If you still don't have 15 Mb, you can choose a minimum installation requiring only 5.5 Mb.)

When you are ready to begin, follow these steps:

1. Start Windows and insert *Startup - Disk 1* into the appropriate floppy-disk drive.

2. Choose File ➤ Run in the Program Manager. The Run dialog box appears.

3. In the Command Line text box enter **A:SETUP** or **B:SETUP** (depending on where you have inserted the Setup disk) and click the OK button.

4. Follow each instruction that appears on the screen. For initialization purposes, the Setup program asks you for some information about yourself. Then you are given the opportunity to specify a drive and directory for the installation; the default is C:\WINWORD. If you have the required disk space, Setup gives you three installation options: Complete Installation, Custom Installation, or Minimum Installation. Click the first of these options to install the entire program.

5. After you have answered all the preliminary questions, the installation begins. Setup tells you when to swap disks and shows you how much of the process has been completed at any given point.

6. When installation is finished, Setup creates the Word for Windows 2.0 program group in the Program Manager. Double-click the Word icon to start the program.

INDEX

U

V

W

Z

Selections from The SYBEX Library

WORD PROCESSING

The ABC's of Microsoft Word (Third Edition)
Alan R. Neibauer
461pp. Ref. 604-9

This is for the novice WORD user who wants to begin producing documents in the shortest time possible. Each chapter has short, easy-to-follow lessons for both keyboard and mouse, including all the basic editing, formatting and printing functions. Version 5.0.

The ABC's of Microsoft Word for Windows
Alan R. Neibauer
334pp. Ref. 784-6

Designed for beginning Word for Windows users, as well as for experienced Word users who are changing from DOS to the Windows version. Covers everything from typing, saving, and printing your first document, to creating tables, equations, and graphics.

The ABC's of WordPerfect 5
Alan R. Neibauer
283pp. Ref. 504-2

This introduction explains the basics of desktop publishing with WordPerfect 5: editing, layout, formatting, printing, sorting, merging, and more. Readers are shown how to use WordPerfect 5's new features to produce great-looking reports.

The ABC's of WordPerfect 5.1 for Windows
Alan R. Neibauer
350pp; Ref. 803-3

This highly praised beginner's tutorial is now in a special new edition for Word-Perfect 5.1 for Windows—featuring WYSI-WYG graphics, font preview, the button bar, and more. It covers all the essentials of word processing, from basic editing to simple desktop publishing, in short, easy-to-follow lessons. Suitable for first-time computer users.

The ABC's of WordPerfect 5.1
Alan R. Neibauer
352pp. Ref. 672-3

Neibauer's delightful writing style makes this clear tutorial an especially effective learning tool. Learn all about 5.1's new drop-down menus and mouse capabilities that reduce the tedious memorization of function keys.

The Complete Guide to MultiMate
Carol Holcomb Dreger
208pp. Ref. 229-9

This step-by-step tutorial is also an excellent reference guide to MultiMate features and uses. Topics include search/replace, library and merge functions, repagination, document defaults and more.

Encyclopedia WordPerfect 5.1
Greg Harvey
Kay Yarborough Nelson
1100pp. Ref. 676-6

This comprehensive, up-to-date Word-Perfect reference is a must for beginning and experienced users alike. With complete, easy-to-find information on every WordPerfect feature and command—and it's organized by practical functions, with business users in mind.

Mastering Microsoft Word on the IBM PC (Fourth Edition)

Matthew Holtz

680pp. Ref. 597-2

This comprehensive, step-by-step guide details all the new desktop publishing developments in this versatile word processor, including details on editing, formatting, printing, and laser printing. Holtz uses sample business documents to demonstrate the use of different fonts, graphics, and complex documents. Includes Fast Track speed notes. For Versions 4 and 5.

Mastering Microsoft Word 5.5 (Fifth Edition)
Matthew Holtz

650pp; Ref. 836-X

This up-to-date edition is a comprehensive guide to productivity with Word 5.5—from basic tutorials for beginners to hands-on treatment of Word's extensive desktop publishing capabilities. Special topics include style sheets, form letters and labels, spreadsheets and tables, graphics, and macros.

Mastering Microsoft Word for Windows
Michael J. Young

540pp. Ref. 619-7

A practical introduction to Word for Windows, with a quick-start tutorial for newcomers. Subsequent chapters explore editing, formatting, and printing, and cover such advanced topics as page design, Style Sheets, the Outliner, Glossaries, automatic indexing, using graphics, and desktop publishing.

Mastering Microsoft Word for Windows (Second Edition)
Michael J. Young

550pp; Ref. 1012-6

Here is an up-to-date new edition of our complete guide to Word for Windows, featuring the latest software release. It offers a tutorial for newcomers, and hands-on coverage of intermediate to advanced topics, with an emphasis on desktop publishing skills. Special topics include tables and columns, fonts, graph-

ics, Styles and Templates, macros, and multiple windows.

Mastering Microsoft Works on the IBM PC
Rebecca Bridges Altman

536pp. Ref. 690-1

Written especially for small business and home office users. Practical tutorials cover every aspect of word processing, spreadsheets, business graphics, database management and reporting, and basic telecommunications under Microsoft Works.

Mastering MultiMate 4.0
Paula B. Hottin

404pp. Ref. 697-9

Get thorough coverage from a practical perspective. Tutorials and real-life examples cover everything from first startup to basic editing, formatting, and printing; advanced editing and document management; enhanced page design, graphics, laser printing; merge-printing; and macros.

Mastering WordPerfect 5
Susan Baake Kelly

709pp. Ref. 500-X

The revised and expanded version of this definitive guide is now on WordPerfect 5 and covers wordprocessing and basic desktop publishing. As more than 200,000 readers of the original edition can attest, no tutorial approaches it for clarity and depth of treatment. Sorting, line drawing, and laser printing included.

Mastering WordPerfect 5.1
Alan Simpson

1050pp. Ref. 670-7

The ultimate guide for the WordPerfect user. Alan Simpson, the "master communicator," puts you in charge of the latest features of 5.1: new dropdown menus and mouse capabilities, along with the desktop publishing, macro programming, and file conversion functions that have made WordPerfect the most popular word processing program on the market.

SYBEX

FREE BROCHURE!

Complete this form today, and we'll send you a full-color brochure of Sybex bestsellers.

Please supply the name of the Sybex book purchased.

_____

How would you rate it?

_____ Excellent   _____ Very Good   _____ Average   _____ Poor

Why did you select this particular book?

_____ Recommended to me by a friend
_____ Recommended to me by store personnel
_____ Saw an advertisement in _____
_____ Author's reputation
_____ Saw in Sybex catalog
_____ Required textbook
_____ Sybex reputation
_____ Read book review in _____
_____ In-store display
_____ Other _____

Where did you buy it?

_____ Bookstore
_____ Computer Store or Software Store
_____ Catalog (name: _____)
_____ Direct from Sybex
_____ Other: _____

Did you buy this book with your personal funds?

_____ Yes   _____ No

About how many computer books do you buy each year?

_____ 1-3   _____ 3-5   _____ 5-7   _____ 7-9   _____ 10+

About how many Sybex books do you own?

_____ 1-3   _____ 3-5   _____ 5-7   _____ 7-9   _____ 10+

Please indicate your level of experience with the software covered in this book:

_____ Beginner   _____ Intermediate   _____ Advanced

Which types of software packages do you use regularly?

_____ Accounting   _____ Databases   _____ Networks

_____ Amiga   _____ Desktop Publishing   _____ Operating Systems

_____ Apple/Mac   _____ File Utilities   _____ Spreadsheets

_____ CAD   _____ Money Management   _____ Word Processing

_____ Communications   _____ Languages   _____ Other _____
                                                                    (please specify)

Which of the following best describes your job title?

_____ Administrative/Secretarial   _____ President/CEO

_____ Director   _____ Manager/Supervisor

_____ Engineer/Technician   _____ Other _____
(please specify)

Comments on the weaknesses/strengths of this book: _____

_____

_____

_____

_____

Name _____

Street _____

City/State/Zip _____

Phone _____

PLEASE FOLD, SEAL, AND MAIL TO SYBEX

SYBEX, INC.
Department M
2021 CHALLENGER DR.
ALAMEDA, CALIFORNIA USA
94501

SYBEX

SEAL

THE TOOLBAR

| 1 | 2 | 3 | 4 | 5 | 6 | 7 | 8 | 9 | 10 | 11 | 12 | 13 | 14 | 15 | 16 | 17 | 18 | 19 | 20 | 21 | 22 |

1. New
2. Open
3. Save
4. Cut
5. Copy
6. Paste
7. Undo
8. Numbered List

9. Bulleted List
10. Unindent
11. Indent
12. Table
13. Text Columns
14. Frame
15. Draw
16. Graph

17. Envelope
18. Spelling
19. Print
20. Zoom Whole Page
21. Zoom 100 Percent
22. Zoom Page Width

THE RIBBON

| Normal | Tms Rmn | 12 | B | I | U | | | | | | | | | ¶ |

| 1 | 2 | 3 | 4 | 5 | 6 | 7 | 8 | 9 | 10 | 11 | 12 | 13 | 14 | 15 |

1. Styles
2. Fonts
3. Points
4. Bold
5. Italics
6. Underline
7. Left Align
8. Center

9. Right Align
10. Justify
11. Left-aligned Tab
12. Centered Tab
13. Right-aligned Tab
14. Decimal Tab
15. Show/Hide ¶